PRAISE FOR *LION*
PREVIOUSLY PUBLISHED
AS *A LONG WAY HOME*

"A remarkable story."

—*The Sydney Morning Herald* (Sydney, Australia)

"I literally could not put this book down. . . . [Saroo's] return journey will leave you weeping with joy and the strength of the human spirit."   —*Manly Daily* (Australia)

"We urge you to step behind the headlines and have a read of this absorbing account. . . . With clear recollections and good old-fashioned storytelling, Saroo . . . recalls the fear of being lost and the anguish of separation."   —*The Weekly Review* (Australia)

Lion

Previously published as
A Long Way Home

Saroo Brierley

with Larry Buttrose

NEW AMERICAN LIBRARY

New York

NEW AMERICAN LIBRARY
Published by Berkley
An imprint of Penguin Random House LLC
375 Hudson Street, New York, New York 10014

Copyright © 2013 by Saroo Brierley
Penguin Random House supports copyright. Copyright fuels creativity, encourages diverse
voices, promotes free speech, and creates a vibrant culture. Thank you for buying an authorized
edition of this book and for complying with copyright laws by not reproducing, scanning, or
distributing any part of it in any form without permission. You are supporting writers and
allowing Penguin Random House to continue to publish books for every reader.

New American Library and the NAL colophon are registered trademarks of
Penguin Random House LLC.

ISBN 9780399584695

The Library of Congress has catalogued the G. P. Putnam's Sons hardcover edition of
A Long Way Home as follows:

A long way home: a memoir/Saroo Brierley with Larry Buttrose.
p.   cm.
ISBN 9780399169281
1. Brierley, Saroo.   2. Brierley, Saroo—Family.   3. Brierley, Saroo—Travel—India.
4. East Indians—Australia—Biography.   5. Adopted children—Australia—Tasmania—
Biography.   6. Birth parents—India—Identification.   7. Intercountry adoption—Australia—
Tasmania.   8. Intercountry adoption—India.   9. Hobart (Tas.)—Biography.   10. Kolkata
(India)—Biography.   I. Buttrose, Larry, 1952-.   II. Title.
CT2808.B67A3   2014   2014003745
920.00920946—dc23

G. P. Putnam's Sons hardcover edition (*A Long Way Home*) / June 2014
Berkley trade paperback edition (*A Long Way Home*) / June 2015
New American Library trade paperback edition (*Lion* movie tie-in edition) / November 2016

Printed in the United States of America
1   3   5   7   9   10   8   6   4   2

Book design by Michelle McMillan

Penguin is committed to publishing works of quality and integrity.
In that spirit, we are proud to offer this book to our readers; however
the story, the experiences and the words are the author's alone.

For Guddu

Contents

Lion

Prologue

They've gone.

I've been thinking about this day for twenty-five years. Growing up half a world away, with a new name and a new family, wondering whether I would ever see my mother and brothers and sister again. And now here I am, standing at a door near the corner of a run-down building in a poor district of a small, dusty town in central India—the place I grew up—and no one lives here. It's empty.

The last time I stood on this ground, I was five years old.

The door, its hinges broken, is so much smaller than I remember it as a child—now I would have to bend over to fit through it. There's no point in knocking. Through the window, as well as some gaps in the familiar crumbling brick wall, I can see into the tiny room my family shared, the ceiling only a little higher than my head.

This was my worst fear, so paralyzing that I suppressed it almost completely—that once I finally found my home, after years of searching, my family wouldn't be in it.

Not for the first time in my life, I'm lost and I don't know what to do. This time I'm thirty, I've got money in my pocket and a ticket to the place I now call home, but I feel just like I did on that railway platform all those years ago—it's hard to breathe, my mind is racing, and I wish I could change the past.

Then the neighbor's door opens. A young woman in red robes comes out of the better-maintained flat next door, holding a baby in her arms. She's curious, understandably. I look Indian, but my Western clothes are probably a little too new, my hair carefully styled—I'm obviously an outsider, a foreigner. To make matters worse, I can't speak her language, so when she speaks to me, I can only guess that she's asking me what I want. I remember barely any Hindi, and I'm not confident about how to pronounce the little I do know. I say, "I don't speak Hindi, I speak English," and I'm astonished when she responds, "I speak English, a little." I point at the abandoned room and recite the names of the people who used to live there—Kamla, Guddu, Kallu, Shekila—and then I point to myself and say, "Saroo."

This time the woman remains silent. Then I remember something Mum gave me back in Australia, for just this situation. I scrabble around in my daypack and pull out a page with color photographs of me as a child. Again I point to myself, and then say "little" as I point to the boy in the photographs. "Saroo."

I try to remember who lived next door to us when this was my home. Was there a little girl who could now be this woman?

She stares at the page, then at me.

I'm not sure if she understands, but this time she speaks, in hesitant English.

"People . . . not live here . . . today," she says.

Although she is only confirming what I know, to hear her say it aloud hits me hard. I feel dizzy. I'm left standing there in front of her, unable to move.

I've always known that even if I managed to find my way back here, my family might have moved. Even in my short time with them, they had moved here from another place. Poor people often don't have much say in where they live, and my mother used to have to take whatever work she could get.

These are the thoughts that start coming out of the box I've put them in. The other possibility—that my mother is dead—I jam back inside.

A man who has noticed us approaches, so I start my mantra over again, reciting the names of my mother, Kamla; my brothers,

Guddu and Kallu; my sister, Shekila; and me, Saroo. He is about to say something when another man wanders up and takes over. "Yes? How can I help?" he says in clear English.

This is the first person I've been able to talk to properly since I arrived in India, and my story comes tumbling out quickly: I used to live here when I was a little boy, I went off with my brother and got lost, I grew up in another country, I couldn't even remember the name of this place, but now I've found my way back here, to Ganesh Talai, to try to find my mother, my brothers, and my sister. Kamla, Guddu, Kallu, Shekila.

He looks surprised at the story, and I recite the family names yet again.

After a moment, he says, "Please wait here. I'll be back in two minutes."

My mind races with possibilities—what has he gone to get? Someone who might know what happened to them? An address, even? But has he understood who I am? I don't have to wait long before he's back. And he says the words I'll never forget:

"Come with me. I'm going to take you to your mother."

1.

Remembering

When I was growing up in Hobart, I had a map of India on my bedroom wall. My mum—my adoptive mother—had put it there to help me feel at home when I arrived from that country at the age of six to live with them in 1987. She had to teach me what the map represented—I was completely uneducated. I didn't even know what a map was, let alone the shape of India.

Mum had decorated the house with Indian objects—there were some Hindu statues, brass ornaments and bells, and lots of little elephant figurines. I didn't know then that these weren't normal objects to have in an Australian house. She had also put some Indian printed fabric in my room, across the dresser, and a carved wooden puppet in a brightly colored outfit. All these things seemed sort of familiar, even if I hadn't seen anything exactly like them before. Another adoptive parent might have made the decision that I was young enough to start my life in Australia with a clean slate and could be brought up without much reference to where I'd come from. But my skin color would always have given away my origins, and anyway, she and my father chose to adopt a child from India for a reason, as I will go into later.

The map's hundreds of place-names swam before me throughout my childhood. Long before I could read them, I knew that the immense V of the Indian subcontinent was a place teeming with cities and towns, with deserts and mountains, rivers and forests—the Ganges, the Himalayas, tigers, gods!—and it came to fascinate me. I would stare up at the map, lost in the thought that somewhere among all those names was the place I had come from, the place of my birth. I knew it was called "Ginestlay," but whether that was the name of a city, or a town, or a village, or maybe even a street—and where to start looking for it on that map—I had no idea.

I didn't know for certain how old I was, either. Although official documents showed my birthday as May 22, 1981, the year had been estimated by Indian authorities, and the date in May was the day I had arrived at the orphanage from which I had been offered up for adoption. An uneducated, confused boy, I hadn't been able to explain much about who I was or where I'd come from.

At first, Mum and Dad didn't know how I'd become lost. All they knew—all anyone knew—was that I'd been picked off the streets of Calcutta, as it was still known then, and after attempts to find my family had failed, I had been put in the orphanage. Happily for all of us, I was adopted by the Brierleys. So to start with, Mum and Dad would point to Calcutta on my map and tell me that's where I came from—but in fact the first time I ever heard the name of that city was when they said it. It wasn't until about a year after I arrived, once I'd made some headway with English, that I was able to explain that I didn't come from Calcutta at all—a train had taken me there from a train station near "Ginestlay." That station might have been called something like "Bramapour," "Berampur" . . . I wasn't sure. All I knew was that it was a long way from Calcutta, and no one had been able to help me find it.

Of course, when I first arrived in Australia, the emphasis was on the future, not the past. I was being introduced to a new life in a very different world from the one I'd been born into, and my new mum and dad were putting a lot of effort into facing the challenges that experience brought. Mum didn't worry too much about my learning English immediately, since she knew it would come through day-to-day use. Rather than trying to rush me into it, she thought it was far more important at the outset to comfort and care for me, and gain my trust. You don't need words for that. She also knew an Indian couple in the neighborhood, Saleen and

Jacob, and we would visit them regularly to eat Indian food together. They would speak with me in my own language, Hindi, asking simple questions and translating instructions and things Mum and Dad wanted me to know about how we'd live our life together. Being so young when I got lost and coming from a very basic background, I didn't speak much Hindi, either, but being understood by someone was a huge help in becoming comfortable about my new surroundings. Anything my new parents weren't able to communicate through gestures and smiles, we knew Saleen and Jacob could help us with, so we were never stuck.

I picked up my new language quite quickly, as children often do. But at first I spoke very little about my past in India. My parents didn't want to push me to talk about it until I was ready, and apparently I didn't show many signs that I gave it much thought. Mum remembers a time when I was seven when out of the blue I got very distressed and cried out, "Me begot!" Later she found out I was upset that I had forgotten the way to the school near my Indian home, where I used to watch the students. We agreed that it probably didn't matter anymore. But deep down, it mattered to me. My memories were all I had of my past, and privately I thought about them over and over, trying to ensure that I didn't "beget."

In fact, the past was never far from my mind. At night, memories would flash by and I'd have trouble calming myself so I could sleep. Daytime was generally better, with lots of activity to distract me, but my mind was always busy. As a consequence of this and my determination not to forget, I have always recalled my childhood experiences in India clearly, as an almost complete picture—my family, my home, and the traumatic events surrounding my separation from them have remained fresh in my mind, sometimes in great detail. Some of these memories were good, and some of them bad—but I couldn't have one without the other, and I couldn't let them go.

My transition to life in another country and culture wasn't as difficult as one might expect, most likely because, compared to what I'd gone through in India, it was obvious that I was better off in Australia. Of course, more than anything, I wanted to find my mother again, but once I'd realized that was impossible, I knew I had to take whatever opportunity came my way to survive. Mum and Dad were very affectionate, right from the start, always giving me lots of cuddles and making me feel safe, secure, loved, and, above all, *wanted*. That meant a lot to a child who'd been lost and had experienced what it was like for no one to care about him. I bonded with them readily, and very soon trusted them completely. Even at the age of six (I would always accept 1981 as the year of my birth), I understood that I had been awarded a rare second chance. I quickly became Saroo Brierley.

Once I was safe and secure in my new home in Hobart, I thought perhaps it was somehow wrong to dwell on the past— that part of the new life was to keep the old locked away—so I kept my nighttime thoughts to myself. I didn't have the language to explain them at first anyway. And to some degree, I also wasn't aware of how unusual my story was—it was upsetting to me, but I thought it was just the kind of thing that happened to people. It was only later, when I began to open up to people about my experiences, that I knew from their reactions it was out of the ordinary.

Occasionally the night thoughts would spill over into the day. I remember Mum and Dad taking me to see the Hindi film *Salaam Bombay!* Its images of the little boy trying to survive alone in a sprawling city, in the hope of returning to his mother, brought back disturbing memories so sharply that I wept in the dark cinema. After that, my parents only took me to fun Bollywood-style movies.

Even sad music of any kind (though particularly classical) could set off emotional memories, since in India I had often heard music emanating from other people's radios. Seeing or hearing babies cry also affected me strongly, probably because of memories of my little sister, Shekila. The most emotional thing was seeing other families with lots of children. I suppose that, even in my good fortune, they reminded me of what I'd lost.

But eventually I began talking about the past. Only a month or so after my arrival, I described to Saleen my Indian family in outline—mother, sister, two brothers—and that I'd been separated from my brother and become lost. I didn't have the resources to explain too much, and Saleen gently let me lead the story to where I wanted it to go rather than pressing me. Gradually, my English improved; we were speaking Hinglish, but we were all learning. I told Mum and Dad a few more things, like the fact that my father had left the family when I was very little. Most of the time, though, I concentrated on the present: I had started going to school, and I was making new friends and discovering a love of sport.

Then one wet weekend just over a year after I'd arrived in Hobart, I surprised Mum—and myself—by opening up about my life in India. I'd probably come to feel more settled in my new life and now had some words to put to my experiences. I found myself telling her more than ever before about my Indian family: about how we were so poor that we often went hungry, and how my mother would have me go around to people's houses in the neighborhood with a pot to beg for any leftover food. It was an emotional conversation, and Mum held me close during our talk. She suggested that together we draw a map of the place I was from, and as she drew, I pointed out where my family's home was on our street, the way to the river where all the kids played, and the bridge under which you walked to get to the train station. We traced the route with our fingers and then drew the home's layout in detail. We put in where each member of my family slept—even the order in which we lay down at night. We returned to the map and refined it as my English improved. But in the whirl of memories brought on by first making that map, I was soon telling Mum about the circumstances of my becoming lost, as she looked at me, amazed, and took notes. She drew a wavy line on the map, pointing to Calcutta, and wrote, "A very long journey."

A couple of months later, we took a trip to Melbourne to visit some other kids who had been adopted from the same Calcutta orphanage as me. Talking enthusiastically in Hindi to my fellow adoptees inevitably brought back the past very vividly. For the first time, I told Mum that the place I was from was called "Ginestlay," and when she asked me where I was talking about, I confidently, if a little illogically, replied, "You take me there and I'll show you. I know the way."

Saying aloud the name of my home for the first time since arriving in Australia was like opening a release valve. Soon after that, I told an even more complete version of events to a teacher I liked at school. For over an hour and a half, she wrote notes, too, with that same amazed expression. Strange as I found Australia, for Mum and my teacher, hearing me talk about India must have been like trying to understand things that had occurred on another planet.

The story I told them was about people and places I'd turned over in my mind again and again since I arrived in Australia, and which I would continue to think about often as I grew up. Not surprisingly, there are gaps here and there. Sometimes I'm unsure of details, such as the order in which incidents occurred, or how many days passed between them. And it can be difficult for me to separate what I thought and felt then, as a child, from what I've come to think and feel over the course of the twenty-seven years that followed. Although repeated revisiting and searching the past for clues might have disturbed some of the evidence, much of my childhood experience remains vivid in my memory.

Back then, it was a relief to tell my story, as far as I understood it. Now, since the life-changing events that sparked after my thirtieth birthday, I am excited by the prospect that sharing my experiences might inspire hope in others.

2.

——————

Getting Lost

Some of my most vivid memories are the days I spent watching over my baby sister, Shekila, her grubby face smiling up at me as we played peekaboo. She always looked at me with adoring eyes, and it made me feel good to be her protector and hero. In the cooler seasons, Shekila and I spent many nights waiting alone in the chilly house like newly hatched chicks in a nest, wondering if our mother would come home with some food. When no one came, I'd get the bedding out—just a few ragged sheets—and cuddle with her for warmth.

During the hot months of the year, my family would join the others with whom we shared the house and gather together outside in the courtyard, where someone played the harmonium and others sang. I had a real sense of belonging and well-being on those long, warm nights. If there was any milk, the women would bring it out and we children got to share it. The babies were fed first, and if any was left over, the older ones got a taste. I loved the lingering sensation of its sticky sweetness on my tongue.

On those evenings, I used to gaze upward, amazed at how spectacular the night sky was. Some stars shone brightly in the darkness, while others merely blinked. I wondered why flashes of light would suddenly streak across the sky for no reason at all, making us "ooh" and "aah." Afterward we would all huddle together, bundled up in our bedding on the hard ground, before closing our eyes in sleep.

That was in our first house, where I was born, which we shared with another Hindu family. Each group had their own side of a large central room with brick walls and an unsealed floor made of cowpats and mud. It was very simple but certainly no chawl—those warrens of slums where the unfortunate families of the megacities like Mumbai and Delhi find themselves living. Despite the closeness of the quarters, we all got along. My memories of that time are some of my happiest.

My mother, Kamla, was a Hindu and my father a Muslim— an unusual marriage at the time, and one that didn't last long. My father spent very little time with us (I later discovered he had taken a second wife), and so my mother raised us by herself.

My mother was very beautiful, slender, with long, lustrous black hair—I remember her as the loveliest woman in the world. She had broad shoulders, and limbs made of iron from all her hard work. Her hands and face were tattooed, as was the custom, and most of the time she wore a red sari. I don't remember much about my father, since I only saw him a few times. I do recall that he wore white from top to bottom, his face was square and broad, and his curly dark hair was sprinkled with gray.

As well as my mother and my baby sister, Shekila, whose name was Muslim, unlike ours, there were also my older brothers, Guddu and Kallu, whom I loved and looked up to. Guddu was tall and slim, with curly black hair down to his shoulders. He was light-skinned, and his face resembled my mother's. Usually he wore short shorts and a white shirt—all our clothes were hand-me-downs from the neighbors, but because of the heat we didn't need much. Kallu was heavier than Guddu, broad from top to bottom, with thin hair. On the other hand, I had short, straight, thick hair, and I was extremely skinny as a child; my face resembled my father's more than my mother's.

When my father did live with us, he could be violent, taking his frustrations out on us. Of course, we were helpless—a lone woman and four small children. Even after he moved out, he wanted to be rid of us altogether. At the insistence of his new wife, he even tried to force us to leave the area so that he could be free of the burden that our presence brought to bear. But my mother had no money to leave, nowhere to live, and no other way to survive. Her small web of support didn't extend beyond our neighborhood. Eventually, my father and his wife quit the area themselves and moved to another village, which improved things for us a bit.

I was too young to understand the separation of my parents. My father simply wasn't around. On a few occasions I found I had been given rubber flip-flops and was told he'd bought new shoes for all of us, but beyond that he didn't help out.

The only vivid memory I have of seeing my father was when I was four and we all had to go to his house to visit his new baby. It was quite an expedition. My mother got us up and dressed, and we walked in the terrible heat to catch the bus. I remember seeing my mother coming toward me from the outdoor ticket booth, her image hazy in the wavering heat emanating from the tarmac. I kept a particular eye on Shekila, who was exhausted by the sizzling temperature. The bus journey was only a couple of hours, but with the walking and waiting, the journey took all day. There was another hour's walk at the other end, and it was dark by the time we reached the village. We spent the night huddled together in the entranceway of a house owned by some people my mother knew (they had no room inside to offer, but the nights were hot and it wasn't unpleasant). At least we were off the streets.

Only the next morning, after we had shared a little bread and milk, I found out that my mother wasn't coming with us—she was not permitted. So we four children were escorted up the road by a mutual acquaintance of our parents to our father's place. My mother would wait at her friend's house.

Despite all this—or perhaps being oblivious to most of it—I was very happy to see my father when he greeted us at the door. We went inside and saw his new wife and met their baby. It seemed to me his wife was kind to us—she cooked us a nice dinner and we stayed the night there. But in the middle of the night, I was shaken awake by Guddu. He said that he and Kallu were sneaking out, and asked if I wanted to come along. But all I wanted to do was sleep. When I woke again, it was to hear my father answering a loud knocking at the front door. A man had seen my brothers running from the village into the open countryside beyond. The man was worried they could be attacked by wild tigers.

I later learned that Guddu and Kallu had attempted to run away that night—they were upset by what was happening in our family and wanted to get away from our father and his other wife. Fortunately, they were found later that morning, safe and sound.

But one problem morphed into another: the same morning, standing in the street, I saw my father approaching and realized that he was chasing after my mother, with a couple of people following behind him. Not far from me, she suddenly stopped and spun on her heel to face him, and they argued and shouted angrily. Quickly they were joined by other people on both sides. Perhaps their personal argument tapped into the tension between Hindus and Muslims, because it quickly turned into a confrontation. The Hindus lined up with my mother, facing the Muslims, who were aligned with my father. Tempers rose very high, and many insults were exchanged. We children gravitated toward our mother, wondering what would happen with all the shouting and jostling. Then, shockingly, my father hurled a small rock that hit my mother on the head. I was right next to her when it struck her and she fell to her knees, her head bleeding. Luckily, this act of violence seemed to shock the crowds, too, cooling tempers rather than exciting them. As we tended to my mother, the crowd on both sides started to drift away.

A Hindu family found the room to take us in for a few days while my mother rested. They told us later that a police officer had taken my father away and locked him up in the cells at the village police station for a day or two.

This episode stayed with me as an example of my mother's courage in turning to face down her pursuers, and also of the vulnerability of the poor in India. Really, it was just luck that the crowds backed off. My mother—and perhaps all of us—could easily have been killed.

Although we weren't brought up as Muslims, after my father

left, my mother moved us to the Muslim side of town, where I spent most of my childhood. She may have felt that we would fare better there, since the neighborhood was a little less destitute. Even after we moved, I don't remember having any religious instruction as a child, other than the occasional visit to the local shrine. But I do remember simply being told one day that I wasn't to play with my old friends anymore because they were Hindus. I had to find new—Muslim—friends. Back then the religions didn't mix, and neither did the people.

When we moved to our new house, we all carried everything we owned, which was only some crockery and bedding. I cradled in my arms small items such as a rolling pin and light pots and pans. I was excited about being in a new place, although I didn't really know what was happening. At that point I didn't understand what religion was. I just saw Muslims as people who wore different garments than Hindus; the men dressed all in white and some had long beards with white hats on their heads.

In our second home, we were by ourselves but in more cramped quarters. Our flat was one of three on the ground level of a red-brick building and so had the same cowpat-and-mud floor we'd had before. Just a single room, it had a little fireplace in one corner and a clay tank in another for water to drink and sometimes wash with. There was one shelf where we kept our sleeping blankets. Only rich people could afford electricity, so we made do with candlelight. I was afraid of the spiders that would crawl along the wall. There were mice, too, but they didn't bother me the way the insects did. The structure was always falling apart a little—my brothers and I would sometimes pull out a brick and peer outside for fun before putting it back in place.

Our town, which I knew as "Ginestlay," was generally hot and dry, except during the heavy rains of the monsoon. A range of large hills in the distance was the source of the river that ran past the old town walls, and in the monsoon, the river would break its banks and flood the surrounding fields. We used to wait for the river to recede after the rains stopped so we could get back to trying to catch small fish in more manageable waters. In town, the monsoon also meant that the low railway underpass filled with water from the stream it crossed and became un-usable. The underpass was a favorite place for the local kids to play, despite the dust and gravel that rained down on us when a train crossed.

Our neighborhood in particular, with its broken and unpaved streets, was very poor. It housed the town's many railway work-ers, and to the more wealthy and highborn citizenry, it was liter-ally on the wrong side of the tracks. There wasn't much that was new, and some of the buildings were tumbling down. Those who didn't live in communal buildings lived in tiny houses like we had: one or two rooms down narrow, twisting alleyways, fur-nished in the most basic way—a shelf here and there, a low wooden bed, and a tap over a drain, perhaps.

The streets were full of cows wandering around, even in the town center, where they might sleep in the middle of the busiest roads. Pigs slept in families, huddled together on a street corner at night, and in the day they would be gone, foraging for whatever they could find. It was almost as if they worked nine to five and clocked off to go home and sleep. Who knew if they belonged to anyone—they were just there. Most people didn't eat pork, as it was considered unclean. There were goats, too, kept by the Muslim families, and chickens pecking in the dust.

Unfortunately, there were also lots of dogs, which scared me—some were friendly, but many were unpredictable or vicious. I was particularly afraid of dogs after I was chased by one, snarling and barking. As I ran away, I tripped and hit my head on a broken tile sticking up from the old pathway. I was lucky not to lose an eye but got a bad gash along the line of my eyebrow, which a neighbor patched up with a bandage. When I'd finally resumed my walk home, I ran into Baba, our local holy man, who would give advice and a blessing to local people. Baba told me never to be afraid of dogs—that they would only bite you if they felt you were scared of them. I tried to keep that advice in mind but remained nervous around dogs on the street. I knew from my mother that some dogs had a deadly disease that you could catch, even if they didn't do worse than nip you. I still don't like dogs, and I've still got the scar.

Since my father wasn't around, my mother had to support us.

Soon after Shekila's birth, she went off to work on building sites. Since she was a strong woman, she was able to do the hard work involved, carrying heavy rocks and stones on her head in the hot sun. She worked six days a week from morning until dusk for a handful of rupees—something like a dollar and thirty cents. This meant that I didn't see very much of her. Often she had to go to other towns for work and could be away for days at a time. It was a great feeling to see her walking up the street after several days' absence. You couldn't miss her since she always wore a red sari. Usually on Saturdays she would come home, and often she brought back some food. Yet she still couldn't earn enough money to provide for herself and four children. At age ten Guddu went to work, too, and his first long shift of about six hours washing dishes in a restaurant earned him less than half a rupee.

We lived one day at a time. There were many occasions when we begged for food from neighbors, or begged for money and food on the streets by the marketplace and around the railway station. Sometimes my mother would send me out in the evening to knock on doors and ask for leftovers. I'd set off with a metal bowl. Some scowling people angrily shouted, "Go away!" while others might have something to give me—perhaps a little kichery, biryani rice (rice layered with meat), or yogurt curry. Occasionally I got a thrashing if I was too persistent.

Once I found a partially broken glass jar near my house. It

had contained mango pickle, but most of it had been scraped out. I decided to use my fingers to get what remained in the jar. I tried to avoid the glass particles, but I was so hungry that I gulped down whatever I could scoop out.

Often when walking around the neighborhood, I would see crockery that had been left outside to be cleaned. I usually checked to see if anything was stuck to the bottom of the pot. Typically any leftover food was covered with flies, which I'd shoo away before devouring whatever remained. Sometimes a dog was hanging around, and I didn't know if it had licked the pot or not. I'd get a rock and chase it away before eating what was left. When you're starving, you aren't too particular about what you put into your mouth. On days when no food was available, you just wouldn't eat.

Hunger limits you because you are constantly thinking about getting food, keeping the food if you do get your hands on some, and not knowing when you are going to eat next. It's a vicious cycle. You want something to fill your stomach, but you don't know how to get it. Not having enough to eat paralyzes you and keeps you living hour by hour instead of thinking about what you would like to accomplish in a day, week, month, or year. Hunger and poverty steal your childhood and take away your innocence and sense of security. But I was one of the lucky ones because I not only survived but learned to thrive.

· · ·

One big impact that our Muslim neighborhood had on my upbringing wasn't pleasant—circumcision at about age three. I don't know why I had to endure it even though we weren't converts to Islam—perhaps my mother thought it wise to go along with some of the local area's customs to keep the peace, or maybe she was told it was a requirement of our living there. For whatever reason, it was done without anesthetic, so it's unsurprisingly one of my clearest and earliest memories.

I was playing outside when a boy came up and told me I was needed at home. When I got there, I found a number of people gathered, including Baba. He told me that something important was going to happen, and my mother told me not to worry, that everything would be all right. Then several men from the neighborhood ushered me into the larger upstairs room of our building. There was a big clay pot in the middle of the room, and they told me to take my shorts off and sit down on it. Two of them took hold of my arms, and another stood behind me to support my head with his hand. The remaining two men held my body down where I sat on top of the clay pot. I had no idea what was going on, but I managed to stay fairly calm—until another man arrived with a razor blade in his hands. I cried out and tried to struggle, but they held me fast as the man deftly sliced. It was very painful but over in seconds. He bandaged me up, and my mother carried me out and took care of me on a bed.

A few minutes later, Kallu went into the upstairs room and the same thing happened to him, but not Guddu. Perhaps he'd already had it done.

That night the neighborhood held a party, with feasting and singing, but Kallu and I could only sit on our rooftop, listening. We weren't allowed to go outside for several days, during which time we were forced to fast and wore only a shirt with no trousers while we recovered.

Begging for food in the Muslim neighborhood provided a more varied diet than we'd had before—we occasionally ate meat, such as goat and chicken. We also got to eat special foods during a festival or party, a marriage or other occasion, which meant we had some fun and a free meal as well. People who weren't invited guests had a separate area where they could sit and eat rice with peanuts or perhaps boondi fried in ghee and served on a banana leaf. I was just happy to have a full stomach for a change.

Another place where we might find a morsel of free food was the Saturday market, which was the largest market in town. People came from everywhere with their farm-grown produce and animals for sale or slaughter. A stall might have a mountain of turmeric on display or a huge mound of peanuts in a pyramid. People were negotiating, selling, and buying. The whole town came alive, and the atmosphere was electric. I found it fascinating, even if it was frustrating not to have one rupee for a small treat. But at times it could be a fruitful place to go begging.

Being the eldest, Guddu felt responsible for our survival, and he was always looking for extra jobs to bring in a little more money. He had been told it was possible to make money hawking things on the railway station platform, so when he was around ten, he started selling toothbrush-and-paste kits to travelers. That landed him in jail because of child labor laws. He was known to local police—as were Kallu and I, and many other young boys in our neighborhood—as a chancer, maybe a petty thief. For example, we had worked out how to cut holes in bales of rice and chickpeas stacked at the station for the cargo trains, to collect some food for our table. Generally, we'd get away or get a clip over the ear, and weren't considered great menaces to society. But for some reason, although Guddu was arrested under laws designed to protect kids, they kept him in jail.

After a few days, a local policeman told my mother where he was. She took us all to the juvenile prison, an imposing complex of buildings packed with young boys, and pleaded with the officers until Guddu was released. I have no idea what she said, but it would have been clear she wasn't leaving without her son. When they walked out of the office to where Shekila and I were waiting, all of a sudden it seemed as if the whole prison gave a big shout—as if to say, "Well done for getting out of this place! You are our hero!" To me it seemed as if he were a celebrity. We were relieved that he was free, but now he had to find new ways to make some money.

Somehow we managed to eke out a subsistence, living day to day and hand to mouth. Everyone in my family used to go out in the morning and get whatever they could—be it money or food. At the end of each day we would return, put whatever we had managed to find on the table, and everyone would share. Sometimes my brothers managed to nab some bhuja, which was chickpea flour mixed with spices. My mother would send us out to borrow some oil, and then she'd deep-fry the dough.

If my mother was able to bring home some yellow lentils, she made dal. First she washed the lentils, then placed them in a pot of boiling water with salt and turmeric, or haldi. When we could, we ate it with green chilis, roti bread, or boiled rice. The roti bread was made from whole wheat flour fresh from the mill. My mother would put a few handfuls of flour into a bowl and mix it with water that we kept in a large clay pot. She mixed it up well and made it into a dough. Then she took little bits from the mound, flattened it out on a board with a rolling pin, and placed it on the preheated iron griddle above the open fire. She cooked both sides of the bread until it started to rise and puff up like a ball, which meant it was ready to eat. But this meal of roti bread and dal was a luxury, and we didn't have it very often.

Once in a while my mother got her hands on some goat gizzards. We always watched her when she cooked, anticipating a rare taste of meat. I remember smelling the ginger and garlic sizzling, the sweet aroma making my mouth water. Then she would add more oil and turmeric, and last the gizzards. She divided up the food, taking less for herself even though she was doing hard manual labor. The savory taste of the garlicky meat exploded in my mouth.

I remember feeling hungry most of the time. There was no choice in the matter; hunger was simply a fact of life, like the searing heat and the constantly buzzing flies. We were very skinny children, with blown-up stomachs from gas and no food. We were malnourished, but then so were other poor children in our village.

As we got older, my brothers and I became more and more creative about finding things to eat. We would roam aimlessly about the neighborhood like vagabonds, hoping to come across a party where there might be some leftovers, or an unwatched vegetable patch or fruit tree. Sometimes it was as simple as throwing stones at blushing ripe mangoes high up in someone's yard, trying to knock one down. On the other side of the village there was a tamarind tree, and I would try to shoot down the reddish pods with a homemade slingshot. Once in a while I might get a handful of the sweet-sour fruit, if other kids hadn't gotten there first.

At other times my brothers and I were more adventurous. One day while walking home, we decided to take a back way through the fields and came across a large henhouse, around fifty meters long. Armed guards were on duty, but Guddu thought we could safely get our hands on some eggs, so we made a plan to stay hidden until the guards went on a tea break. Then I would go into the henhouse first, being shorter and harder to spot, and Guddu and Kallu would follow. Guddu told us to roll up our shirts inside out so that they could serve as little baskets. We were to quickly collect as many eggs as we could, then run out and go straight back home.

We watched from a hideout until the guards' break, when they went to sit with the shed workers, eating rotis and drinking chai. There was no time to waste. I was the first inside and started grabbing the brown speckled eggs, still warm from the hens' undersides. Guddu and Kallu followed and did the same. But the chickens became disturbed by our presence and started squawking loudly, alerting the guards. We dashed back out as the guards ran toward the shed, only about twenty meters from us. Guddu yelled, "Run for it!" and we split up and bolted. We were a lot faster than the guards, and luckily they chose not to shoot at us. Unfortunately, the act of running had not been kind to my eggs; of the nine I'd collected, only two remained intact— the rest were dripping down my shirtfront.

My brothers had beaten me home and my mother had the

iron griddle on the flame. Between us we had ten eggs left—enough to feed us all. My stomach rumbled as I watched my mother put two delicious-smelling fried eggs on an aluminum plate. I thought, *I hope she gives me the first batch,* but instead she gave it to Shekila. I couldn't help myself—I nabbed an egg from my sister's plate and ran out the door, ignoring her earsplitting cry of protest. I didn't get punished, probably because my mother realized how ravenous I was.

On another occasion I woke early feeling very hungry, but there was nothing to eat in the house. I remembered having noticed a field of ripening tomatoes nearby, and went out determined to lay my hands on some. It was cool in the early morning air, and I still had my sleeping blanket wrapped around me. When I reached the field, I squeezed in through a gap in the barbed-wire fence and within moments I was picking tomatoes, eating some on the spot, savoring their soft flesh. But then I heard a whistle blow loudly and saw a group of five or six older boys running quickly toward me across the field. I dashed back to the fence and, being little, managed to squeeze through an opening I knew would be too small for them. But my prized red blanket got snagged on the barbed wire, and with the boys bearing down on me, I had to leave it behind. When I got home my mother was happy I had brought some tomatoes to eat, but furious I had lost my blanket in the process. She didn't beat me like a lot of parents did, though; she never raised a hand to any of us, instead disciplining us only by scolding.

Our landlady, who lived in our building, often cooked kichery, which was rice and lentil curry. She would prepare all the ingredients and put them in a pot to cook, and then leave her house to visit friends for a while. My nose was very sensitive to the scent of food since I was hungry just about all of the time, and one morning it led me to an intoxicating spicy smell emanating from our landlady's kitchen. I crept into the room and had a vision of heaven: a fresh pot of kichery, simmering away untended.

I went up to the pot, opened the lid, and stared at the feast, my mouth watering uncontrollably. I put my finger into it to see if it was too hot, but luckily for me it was still lukewarm. Quickly I scooped up a handful and gulped the delicious cumin-savory lentils, taking several scoops until my belly was full. Then with my palm I flattened the top of the curry so it looked untouched, licked my hand clean, and snuck back out of the room. Apparently I got away with it, because our landlady never complained.

Another run-in involving food almost cost me my life. I accepted a job ferrying ten large watermelons across the town's main street for a man with a stall in the town market. He offered me a little money, and I hoped he might add a slice of watermelon when I was done. But the watermelons were very large and I was still small, and struggling with the first one, I wasn't able to keep track of the heavy traffic. The next thing I knew, I was lying on the tarred road, bleeding from the head, with the watermelon next to me crushed into crimson pulp. I was lucky my head had not been crushed in the same way, as I'd been struck by a speeding motorcycle and gone under its wheel. However, my leg was injured. The rider took pity on me and gave me a lift home, and I limped into my house. My mother was horrified and took me straight to a doctor, who bandaged my injuries. I don't know how she paid for it.

Only once did I ever see food being given away to a large group of people off the street. I'd been trying to beg something from a man. He refused but told me that a laundry shop fed the poor once a month. "In fact, if you go there now, you might get some," he said. I hurried to the shop and, sure enough, there was a line of people waiting to be served. However, the woman ahead of me told me that you had to have a bowl. I could see that the steaming curry would be too hot to hold in my hands, so I frantically searched for a container, but to no avail. Finally I found a plastic bag lying on the side of the road. I resumed my place in line, and when I reached the shop owner, he gave me a big spoonful, which made my pangs recede for a while.

Harsh as all this sounds, we learned to live with hunger. We had to; it was always there, like the dirt under our bare feet. The one thing I craved—other than a full stomach—was to attend school as the other kids did. Often, first thing in the morning, I would go and hang around by the gates of the local school as the uniformed children marched in. I would stare inside, wishing I could be a pupil there like them. But in India school isn't free, and we couldn't afford to go. It made me a bit shy, because it was obvious I had no education. I couldn't read or write, and didn't know many words—I spoke poorly and had trouble communicating.

As we grew up, my brothers spent more time away from "Ginestlay" in search of new hunting grounds and sleeping away from the house in railway stations and under bridges. Sometimes the holy man, Baba, would look after Shekila and me at the mosque, or he would take me fishing in the river with his long bamboo stick and line. I always looked forward to being with Baba; he was closer to a father than my real one, whom I never saw. We would walk together to his favorite fishing spots, where he'd put a worm on the hook and cast it into the water. We caught a type of small fish that had black scales, and he always let me bring a few home. Whenever my mother returned from work, she'd cook it in a delicious curry that would make me drool with anticipation. On other days Baba let me watch him clean and decorate the holy place at the tomb. During special festivals, he would choose two boys to be dressed up as tigers. I always wanted to be a tiger and was disappointed when he didn't choose me.

Sometimes it felt as if the world had forgotten about us and our problems. But then we would meet someone from the neighborhood who treated us with respect, like Baba, and who fed us just because he felt sorry for us. When Baba gave me a snack and asked me what I wanted to be when I grew up, he wasn't just nourishing my mind but also my spirit. He gave me a sense of being normal for a few moments, and helped me to believe that I had a future. He gave me the luxury to think about what I wanted to accomplish with my life, either working in the construction area or being a laborer in a shop.

The other person who was a father figure to me for a brief time was one of the supervisors of the young men's military school camp. He noticed me hanging about and would call me over in the morning to share some of the porridge that was made in vast quantities for the boys at the camp. The porridge was such a delicacy to me, as only well-off people could afford it. To this day I can still taste and smell its comforting flavor. The supervisor was very kind and took an avuncular interest in me, asking me what I'd been doing the day before and teaching me how to whistle. The highlight was when he gave me and some other kids a ride in the back of his jeep to pick up someone at the train station. I was sad when he moved away and I never saw him again.

. . .

Another bright spot in my existence was the cinema, but the only way I could get into it was to sneak through when no one was watching. Sometimes I'd make it inside, only to be chucked out because they could tell just by looking at me that I hadn't paid. Occasionally my brothers and I got to see an entire movie, and I fell in love with the drama and music. My favorite actor was Mithun Chakraborty, and the best song I ever heard was "Lambi Judai."

Since Guddu and Kallu were spending less and less time in our neighborhood, Shekila became the person I was closest to. When she was around a year old and I was a certain age, probably about four, I was responsible for her welfare. My duties were to wash and feed her, and watch over her. Shekila and I used to sleep in the same bed, and when we woke, I would fetch her whatever breakfast I could find. We used to play together: peekaboo and hide-and-seek. Shekila was so tiny and beautiful. She had short, curly hair and was usually dressed in a dirty white frock. She loved being with me and followed me everywhere, and I protected her and was always on alert to hear if anyone had mistreated her. Shekila was my main priority, as much as a very young child can have a sense of that sort of responsibility.

Although Guddu was the oldest, Kallu played a similar role

with him. As Guddu worked a few jobs at different times to help with the family income, Kallu took care of him because he was one of our breadwinners—the younger brother would ensure that the elder was getting enough to eat and that if they both stayed away from home, the elder had a safe place to sleep. So with no father around, and our mother often away working, we took care of each other.

For the most part, while the other kids my age were in school and I was watching Shekila, I stuck to the boundaries of the house and its courtyard. I spent long days sitting on the earthen floor alone while she slept, idly listening in on conversations and watching life go on around me. Sometimes the neighbors kept an eye on her and let me go off and find wood for cooking. I would haul it back and stack it by the side of the house.

I also earned a paisa or two—enough for a lollipop, some sugarcane, or another small bit of food—by helping the local storekeeper with his deliveries of wooden planks. He'd have me stack them in the pen by the store's front door. I had to place each piece of wood neatly so it didn't overflow and fall into the walkway. It took two hours to get the job done, and I'd wind up with a few splinters. At the end I had to clean the entire area right down to the small chips. Sometimes other kids would show up and the job would get done more quickly, but that meant I only got a third or a quarter of the payment.

But most of the time I simply sat alone in our courtyard. We had no TV or radio. There were no books or newspapers, although I couldn't have read them anyway. It was a simple, basic existence, and much of it was spent in trying to find something to put into my and Shekila's ever-complaining stomachs.

When she was two, Shekila discovered an unusual and unhealthy way to appease her constant hunger pangs. At times I caught her eating charcoal from our fireplace. She would hide small chunks of it in the hem of her dress and furtively gnaw on it, her face blackened by the dust. She became addicted to it, and I'd know she had been eating it when I found black poo in back of our house. It had a terrible effect on her digestive system, and several times we had to take her to a woman who had some special knowledge about how to fix the problem. Then my mother would carry her home wrapped in sheets. I followed behind, feeling relieved that she would be all right.

In the afternoons after school, kids would run around in the streets. Sometimes I'd leave Shekila napping and join them, playing cricket on whatever patch of bare earth we could use. I also loved to chase butterflies, and glow bugs when it got darker. Flying kites was another favorite pastime. The kites were simple—sticks and paper—but to own even a basic kite required a little money. The rich kids had amazingly big, patterned ones, some even with colorful bows on the tails. I was mad for a kite like theirs, so I'd try to spot one stuck in a tree and climb up and get it, no matter how dangerous it was. Guddu showed me how to make my own; you just laid two sticks in a cross on a piece of paper and sewed it together with cotton string. We conducted some exciting kite dogfights, for which we would stick crushed glass to our kite's string, giving it an abrasive cutting edge. We would try to cut the string of the other's kite as it flew. Kids played marbles, too, but again you needed money to get a marble to start with.

I didn't really have any close friends—maybe it was because of our being Hindu in a Muslim neighborhood. I also had the sense that some kids had been told not to associate with us because we were so poor. In addition, society held my mother in disgrace because her husband had left her. For these reasons and also perhaps from being chased away so many times while begging, I had a general mistrust of those I didn't already know well—so I hung out as much as possible with my brothers, whom I adored.

As I got a bit older, I was given more leeway outside the house and was allowed to start playing farther away. To begin with I stayed close to home, so that if anything bad happened I could run down this or that street, take a quick turn, and be home. Eventually, though, I started venturing as far as the town center, or my brothers and I would go down to the river below the dam wall, a long walk away, beyond the edge of town. We'd watch fishermen using their nets to catch fish.

One memorable day a helicopter landed near the field of the

nearby military school, and everyone ran over to see what was going on. I didn't know what it was, but I was intrigued by the fact that something that big could fly. From that time on, I was fascinated by anything in the sky. I tried to figure out why large birds could soar yet I couldn't. I'd see a vapor trail, tracing a thin white line among the clouds, and hope that one day I'd get to see what created it.

A group of Hindu kids played hide-and-seek near the temple, and I would join them for hours, even though there weren't a lot of places to hide. During the hot season, swarms of tiny glow bugs came out at dusk. We'd catch them in our hands and then let them go, amazed by the flickering light they put out. I enjoyed the company of these kids, but one night when I showed up, I was told I couldn't play with them anymore, probably because they'd discovered I lived on the Muslim side of town. At first I was devastated, but eventually I got over it and found other pastimes. I'd leave Shekila at the house for a while, knowing she could safely pass the time by herself while I was out. I'm sure this is illegal in the West, but in my town it wasn't uncommon when parents had other things to do, and I'd been left like that many times myself.

Once during my rambles I got lucky: a shop owner asked if I could peel the potatoes for pani puri, which is a puffed, crisp, savory treat that is fried, submerged in cold spiced water, and then eaten. The man sat me down with a big bowl of potatoes, and I started peeling. It took ages, and he told me not to eat any or he would send me packing without my payment—which was to be six of the cooked pani puri. Even though the owner kept a sharp eye on me as he was going about his business, I still managed to furtively pop a few pieces into my mouth, and they seemed to melt on my tongue.

It was torture to handle such appetizing food and not be able to eat it. When the man turned his back for a moment, I decided to risk it one more time and slipped what I thought was a small piece of potato into my mouth. The burning sensation told me that I had accidentally eaten a chunk of salt that had fallen into the bowl. I was dying of thirst, but I knew I couldn't ask for water, and somehow I managed to continue peeling the rest of the potatoes. After I had finished, he made up the dough and cooked the delicacies. I was paid my six pani puri, and thus managed to fill my stomach and also Shekila's.

By the time Guddu and Kallu were about fourteen and twelve, respectively, they were spending very little time at home. I didn't see them more than two or three times a week. They were mostly living off their wits, scouring the streets for whatever they could find to subsist on and sleeping nights in railway stations, where they sometimes earned food or money for sweeping. Most of the time they stayed at another town a few stops down the train line, about an hour away. They would tell me "Ginestlay" was no good, so they were going to a place that sounded like "Berampur"—at the time, I could never remember its name. Apparently it was easier to find money and food there, and they had started making friends, too, all of them getting around by jumping on and off trains.

When I got to be about four or five, occasionally my brothers would take me along with them. If a conductor ever asked for a ticket, we simply got off and hopped on the next train. We'd pass through a couple of very small stations—just platforms in the middle of nowhere—before arriving at the "Berampur" station, smaller than the one at "Ginestlay" and on the outskirts of town. I would beg for money, saying, *"Eka rupaya"*—"one rupee"—or just stand behind someone until he either gave me something or chased me away. I found that if you tapped a person lightly on the side, you'd find out more quickly if they would give you something or not. But my brothers would only let me go as far as the station; I couldn't go wandering off into the town, where I might get lost. So I'd hang around the platforms while they worked, then go back home with them.

Some nights we played hide-and-seek in the cargo carriages that had been off-loaded, which could have been very dangerous if a speeding train had gone by, as often we were running between tracks. Once when we were playing, a policeman shooed us off and told us never to come back. We simply moved our game to another part of town. My brothers and I often didn't have food, but we had freedom, and we liked it.

One night, when I was five years old, I was at home, tired from a day playing out in the streets, but excited that on this night almost the whole family was gathered for dinner. My mother was home from work and, more unusually, Guddu was there, too. Kallu was the only one missing.

That evening, Guddu stayed for about an hour while the four of us ate together. As Guddu was the eldest, it was he that I looked up to the most. He hadn't been home for some time, and I missed hanging out with him and Kallu as a gang. I'd begun to feel I wasn't a little boy anymore, to be left at home while they were out in the world.

After dinner, when our mother went out (perhaps to see if she could get us some more food), Guddu announced that he was leaving—going back to "Berampur." The thought of once again being left behind without my brother, a little kid stuck at home with nothing to do, was too much. I jumped up and said, "I'm coming with you!" It was early evening—if I went with him, there was little likelihood of him getting me back home that night. We'd have to stay together. He thought about it for a moment and then agreed. I was thrilled. We left Shekila sitting on the floor and were gone before my mother returned. She probably wouldn't have been too worried, with me in my brother's care.

Soon I was laughing as we sped through the night, Guddu doubling me on a bike through the quiet streets to the train station. A man who lived beyond the center of town hired out bicycles for less than one paisa, and sometimes Guddu rented one to get to and from his jobs more quickly.

I'd traveled with my brothers before, but that night was different. I was going off with Guddu without a plan for when we were coming home or where we might sleep, just like he did with Kallu. I didn't know how long he would let me stay with him, but as we raced through the streets, I didn't care.

I still vividly remember the ride. I sat on the bar just behind the bike's handlebars with my feet resting on either side of the front-wheel axle. It was a bumpy trip, as there were potholes everywhere in the road, but I didn't mind at all. There were a lot of glow bugs flying in the air, and we passed some kids chasing them. A boy yelled out, "Hey, Guddu!" but we rode on. I was proud that Guddu was known about town. I had even heard him mentioned once when I was on a train—I thought he was famous. We had to keep a good lookout for people walking on the street in the dark, especially when we went under the low railway bridge. Then Guddu said we'd walk the rest of the way;

maybe he was tired with me on board. So I hopped off and he pushed the bike along the main street to the station, past the busy chai sellers. When we were near the station entrance, Guddu hid the hire bike behind some thick bushes, and we walked across the overpass to wait for the next train.

By the time the train noisily pulled in and we had scuttled aboard, I was already becoming sleepy. We got as comfortable as we could on the hard wooden seats, but the fun of the adventure was starting to wear off. I rested my head on Guddu's shoulder as the train left the station. It was getting late, and we'd be on the train for about an hour. I don't know if Guddu was having second thoughts about letting me come, but I was starting to feel a bit guilty, because my mother usually needed me to babysit Shekila while she was at work, and I didn't know when I'd be back.

By the time we got off at "Berampur," I was so exhausted that I slumped onto a wooden bench on the platform and said I couldn't go on without a rest. Guddu said that was fine—there were a few things he needed to do anyway. "Just sit down and don't move. I'll come back in a little while and we can find somewhere to sleep the night." I lay down, shut my eyes, and must have fallen asleep straightaway.

When I woke up, it was very quiet and the station was deserted. Bleary-eyed, I looked around for Guddu but couldn't see him anywhere. There was a train at the platform where we'd got off, with its carriage door open, but I didn't know if it was the same one, or how long I'd been asleep.

I've often wondered exactly what I was thinking right then. I was still half-asleep and I remember being unnerved by finding myself at the station alone at night. My thoughts were muddled. Guddu wasn't around, but he'd said he wasn't going far—maybe he'd got back on the train? I shuffled over and climbed the boarding stairs to have a look. I have a memory of seeing some people asleep on board and stepping back down from the carriage, worried that if they woke up, they would call the conductor. Guddu had said I should stay put, but he was probably on board in a different carriage, working, sweeping underneath the seats. What if I fell asleep on the dark platform again and the train pulled out and I was left alone?

I looked into a different carriage and found no one, but the empty wooden bench seats were more comfortable and felt safer than the quiet station—Guddu would come and get me soon, smiling, perhaps with a treat he'd found while cleaning. There was plenty of room to stretch out. In a few moments, I was sleeping peacefully again.

This time, I must have slept properly. When I awoke, it was broad daylight and the full sun was glaring straight into my eyes. And, I realized with a jolt, the train was moving—rattling steadily along on its tracks.

I jumped up. There was still no one in the carriage, and the landscape outside the barred windows was passing quickly. My brother was nowhere to be seen. I had been left undisturbed, a small boy asleep, alone on a speeding train.

The low-class carriages weren't connected to each other with internal doors. Travelers boarded and exited their carriage from doors on the outside at each end. I raced to one end of the carriage and tried the doors on either side—they were both locked, or wouldn't budge. I ran down to the other end—the doors there were locked, too.

I can still feel the icy chill of panic that hit me when I realized that I was trapped—at once a feeling of weakness, hyperactivity, and incredulity. I don't recall exactly what I did in that moment—screamed, banged the windows, cried, cursed. I was frantic, my heart beating triple time. I couldn't read any of the signs in the carriage. I ran up and down and looked beneath all the benches, in case someone else was asleep somewhere. There was only me. But I kept running up and down, yelling out my brother's name, begging him to come and get me. I called for my mother, and my brother Kallu, too, but all in vain. No one answered and the train didn't stop.

I was lost.

Slowly, I found myself shrinking from the enormity of what confronted me, hunching up into a protective ball. For long hours, I either cried or sat in a quiet daze.

After hurtling along in the empty carriage for a long time, I roused myself to look out the window to see if I could recognize some landmarks. The world outside looked similar to the outskirts of my village, but there were no distinguishing features. I didn't know where I was headed, but I'd traveled much farther than ever before and was already far away from home.

I entered some kind of hibernating state—my system shut down, I suppose, exhausted at trying to deal with what was happening. I wept and slept, and occasionally looked out the window. There was nothing to eat, but there was water to drink from the tap in the filthy toilet cubicles at the rear, with their pitholes open to the tracks below.

Once, I woke up to realize that we'd stopped—we'd pulled into a station. My spirits soared, as I thought I could catch someone's attention on the platform. But there wasn't a soul to be seen in the gloom. I still couldn't budge the exit doors. I beat them with my fists and screamed and screamed as the train gave a lurch and started moving again.

Eventually, I was spent. You can't remain in a state of sheer panic and terror indefinitely, and both had run their course. Ever since, I've thought that must be why we cry: our bodies are coping with something our minds and hearts can't absorb by themselves. I suppose all of that crying had served its purpose—I'd let my body work through my feelings, and now, surprisingly, my mind began to feel a little better. I was exhausted by the experience and fell in and out of sleep. When I think back now and relive the full horror of being trapped alone, with no idea where I was or where I was heading, it's like a nightmare. I remember it in snapshots—awake at the windows, terrified; curled up and drifting in and out of sleep. *Where did Guddu go? Why did he leave me? Why isn't he on this train? Where is it taking me? I want to be with my mother! Where is my sister, where is my brother—where is my home?* I think the train pulled into some more stations, but the doors never opened, and no one ever saw me.

But as time passed—perhaps even twelve hours—some of the resilience I'd built up when exploring my own town started to reassert itself. I began to think, *If I can't get out by myself, then I'll just have to wait until someone lets me out, and then work out how to get home.* I would behave like my brothers would behave. They were away for days at a time; I could do that, too. They had shown me how to find a place to sleep, and I had looked after myself before, finding things and begging. And maybe if this train took me away from home, it could take me back there.

Gradually, over what might have been six or more hours, the countryside became greener than I'd ever seen it before. There were lush fields and tall trees with no branches but great shaggy bunches of fronds at their tops. When the sun came out from behind clouds, everything exploded into bright green light. I saw monkeys running through the tangled undergrowth by the sides of the tracks, and amazing brightly colored birds. There was water everywhere, in rivers, lakes, ponds, and fields. It was a new world to me. Even the people looked a little different: sharper, taller, and lighter in complexion.

After a while, the train began to pass through small towns, and I saw kids playing by the tracks while their mothers cooked or did the laundry on the back stoop. No one seemed to notice a lone child at the window of the passing train. The towns got bigger and closer together, and then there were no more fields, no more open country, just more and more houses—streets and streets of them—roads and cars and rickshaws. There were big buildings, too, many more of them than at home, and buses and trucks and tracks with other trains running along them. Everywhere there were people and more people—more than I had ever seen, more than I could ever have imagined in one place.

Eventually, the train slowed, and I knew it must be approaching another station. Was my journey at an end this time? The train coasted until it was hardly moving at all, then gave a sudden lurch and stopped altogether. Wide-eyed, staring from behind the bars of the window, I saw crowds of people swarming on the platform, hefting luggage as they strode about. People were rushing everywhere, in the hundreds, perhaps thousands, and suddenly someone opened one of the doors to my carriage. Without a moment's thought, I ran down the aisle as fast as I could and leaped out onto the platform. At last I was free.

Only later, from the safety of my bedroom in Hobart, when my parents pointed it out on the wall map, did I find out the name of the city I'd traveled to. Not that it would have meant anything to me at the time. But I had arrived in what was then known as Calcutta, the sprawling megacity famous for its over-population, pollution, and crushing poverty—one of the most dangerous cities in the world.

I stepped off the train truly with nothing but the clothes I was wearing, barefoot, in a grimy pair of black shorts and a white short-sleeved shirt with several buttons missing. I had no money, no food, and no identification of any sort. I was hungry, but I was used to that, so it wasn't too much of a problem yet. What I really hungered for was help.

I was thrilled to be free of my carriage prison but frightened out of my wits by the huge station with its pressing crowds. Frantically, I looked around in the hope of seeing Guddu push-ing past all the people to come and rescue me, as if he might have been stuck on the train, too. But there were no familiar faces. I was paralyzed. I had no idea where to go or what to do. I instinctively stepped out of people's way. I called out, "Ginest-lay? Berampur?" hoping that someone would tell me how to get there. But no one in the rushing mass paid me the slightest attention.

At some point, the train I'd arrived on must have pulled away again, but I don't remember noticing. Even if I had, I doubt I would have been too keen to jump back aboard after being trapped for so long. I was scared into inaction, afraid that wandering off somewhere would make things worse. I kept to the platform, occasionally calling out, "Berampur?"

All around me was a confusion of noise, with people shouting and calling to one another or huddled in babbling conversation— I couldn't understand what anyone was saying. Mostly they were just very busy, pushing on and off trains in the great crush, struggling to get to wherever they needed to be as quickly as possible.

A small handful of people stopped to listen to me, but all I could manage to say to them was something like "Train, Ginestlay?" Most just shook their head and walked on.

One man replied, "But Ginestlay is where?"

I didn't know what he meant; it was just . . . *home*. How could I explain where it was? After a moment, he frowned and moved on. There were a lot of children begging or hanging around the station looking for whatever they could find, as my brothers did back home. I was just one more poor kid crying something out, too small and timid to make anyone stop and listen.

I steered clear of policemen out of habit. I was afraid they might lock me up, as they'd once done to Guddu. Conductors, police, anyone in uniform—we'd avoided them all. It didn't occur to me that now they might be able to help.

I stayed on the platform even after everyone had left, having failed to get anyone's attention, sleeping on and off, unable to move away or think of what to do next. Sometime the next day, tired and miserable, I gave up trying to find help. The people in the station weren't people at all but a great solid mass I couldn't make any impact on, like a river or the sky.

One thing I knew was that if a train had brought me to where I was, a train could take me back. I also knew that at home the trains on the track opposite the one you arrived on went back the other way. But I'd noticed that this station was the end of the line, where all the trains came in and stopped, and then chugged back the way they had come. If no one could tell me where the trains went, I would find out for myself.

So I boarded the next train that arrived at the platform. Could it be as simple as that?

As the train rumbled out, I got a better look at the station from which I had departed: it was a huge red building with many arches and towers, the biggest building I'd ever seen. I was in awe of its size but hoped I was leaving it and its great crush of people behind forever. However, after an hour or so, the train came to the end of its own line, somewhere on the outskirts of the city. Then it switched direction and went back to the enormous station.

I tried another train, but the same thing happened. Maybe the train I needed left from another platform? There were many more platforms here than at the station near home, and each seemed to have several different kinds of trains—some had lots of compartments with porters helping people on, while others had carriage after carriage filled with people on bench seats, like the one that had brought me here. The sheer number of them was frightening, but one of them must go back to where I'd come from—I just had to keep trying.

And so that's what I did. Every day—day after day—I caught a different train out of the city.

To avoid being locked in a carriage again, I only traveled during the day. At the beginning of each trip I would watch the passing scenery with hopeful optimism, thinking, *Yes, yes, this feels like the one that will get me home, I've seen that building or those trees before.* . . . Sometimes the train would reach the end of its journey and then head back again. Other times it simply stopped at the final station on the line, and I'd be stuck in that unfamiliar, empty place until the next day, when the train began the return leg. The only times I got off a train before it reached the end of its journey were when night was falling. Then I'd crawl under the seats inside the station so that I couldn't be easily seen, and curl up tightly for warmth. Luckily, the weather was never very cold.

I survived by eating scraps of food I found on the ground, like peanuts travelers had dropped or corncobs not completely eaten. Sometimes I dove for food that had just been dropped, but then I was risking a kick in the head from the other kids who were hanging around. Fortunately, it wasn't hard to find taps for a drink. This wasn't too different from the way I'd lived before, so although I was often scared and miserable, at least I knew how to get by, and I suppose my system was used to the lack of nourishing food. I was learning how to live on my own.

And so I shuttled back and forth, trying different platforms, traveling different routes—sometimes seeing something I recognized and realizing I'd accidentally caught a train I'd tried before—and in the end not getting anywhere at all.

On each of those journeys not one person ever asked me for a ticket. Of course, I avoided trains when I could see they had conductors on them, just like we did at home, but once I was on, I was never questioned. If an official had stopped me, I might have summoned the courage to try to ask for help, but none ever did. Once, a porter appeared to understand that I was lost, but when I couldn't immediately make myself understood, he made it clear I wasn't to bother him anymore. The world of adults was closed to me, so I continued to try to solve my problem by myself.

After a while, though—perhaps even a couple of weeks—I began to lose heart. Often I thought about my family, especially my brother. Sometimes at night when I was trying to get comfortable on a hard bench, feeling afraid to fall asleep, I would cry to myself, "Where are you, Guddu? Please help me. Take me away from this place. I want to be with you and everyone else." My home was out there somewhere, but maybe no train from here went there. Or maybe there was some sort of complication I couldn't work out. All I knew about the city outside of the station was what I'd seen from train windows, arriving or leaving. Maybe out there was someone who could help me, give me directions to get home, or even just give me some food.

But by now I was growing more and more familiar with the sprawling red station. It felt like my only real connection with where I'd come from, whereas the masses of people coming and going outside frightened me. Each time I went on a trip to a new and strange place, I was glad to get back to the big station, where I knew my way around and knew where to sleep, and where I was most likely to find food. Of course, more than anything, I still wanted to find my mother, but I was slowly adjusting to life at the station.

I had noticed a group of children who seemed to always be at the end of a particular platform, where they'd huddle together in some old blankets at night. They seemed to be like me, with nowhere to go, but they didn't try to hide under seats or on trains. I'd watched them, and they had probably seen me, but they had shown no interest in my presence. I hadn't been confident enough to approach them, but my lack of trust was worn down by my failure to find home. Adults had proven to be of no assistance, but maybe other children would help? At least they might let me stay near them, and perhaps I'd be safer with more kids around.

The children weren't welcoming, but they didn't chase me off, either, as I lay on a hard wooden seat close to them and rested my head on my hands. Kids on their own were not an uncommon sight here, and one more addition to their ranks didn't surprise anyone. Exhausted from the day's train travels but a little relieved with my decision not to start all over again the next day and more secure with the others nearby, I quickly fell asleep.

Before long, though, I was disturbed by what at first I thought was a bad dream. I heard young voices screaming out, "Go away, let me go!" More shouting followed, in both young and older voices, and in the dim light from the station I thought I could make out a man yelling something like "You are coming with me!" Then a child unmistakably screamed out, "RUUUNN!" and I leaped to my feet, knowing that this was no dream.

In the confusion, I saw children being lifted by adult hands and carried off, and a small girl struggling with a man by the edge of a platform. I ran for my life, sprinting away down a darkened platform and leaping off the end of it, down onto the tracks, before charging into the darkness.

Running virtually blind alongside a large wall, I kept looking over my shoulder to see if I was being chased but didn't slow down even when I thought there was no one behind me. I didn't know what had happened back at the station, why the men were grabbing the kids. All I knew was there was no way I was going to get caught myself.

But there was danger ahead as well as behind.

As the track turned to the right, I found myself face-to-face with the blinding lights of a train coming straight at me. I jumped to one side as it hurtled by with a deafening roar, terrifyingly close to my body. I had to press myself as hard as I could against the wall for what felt like an eternity as the train kept passing, with my face shoved sideways to keep clear of anything that might be sticking out from a carriage.

Once the train had passed, I had the chance to recover. Although I was terrified at the dangers in this new city, I'd lived by my wits for long enough not to lose them now. I suppose the advantage of being a naïve five was that I didn't think too much about what had happened to the other children, or what it meant, other than that I wanted to avoid it. What choice did I have but to keep going?

I continued to follow the tracks but more cautiously. When they came to a road, I left them—and the station—for the first time on foot since I'd arrived. The road was busy, which felt safer than being somewhere out of sight, and soon led to the bank of a huge river over which stretched a massive bridge, dark against the gray sky. I remember distinctly the overwhelming impression the sight made on me. I'd seen a few bridges from the windows of trains, bigger than the only one I knew from home, which crossed the little river I played in with my brothers.

In the gaps between the shop stalls huddled along the top of the riverbank, I could see the wide expanse of water, busy with boats. The bridge loomed over it, an immense structure, with people teeming along its walkway, and a slow but noisy mass of bicycles, motorbikes, cars, and trucks on its road. It was an astonishing sight for a little boy from a small village. How many people were here? Was this the biggest place in the world? The opening up of the city beyond the station made me feel more lost than ever.

I stayed on the street for some time, stunned by the scale of the scene before me. While I seemed invisible, I worried that I could come to the attention of people like the men I'd just escaped—or even the very same men, who might still be chasing me. Those thoughts gave me the courage to walk past the shop stalls and between some larger buildings, toward the riverbank. The steep grassy slopes, shaded by big leafy trees, quickly gave way to the muddy river's edge, and the whole area was full of activity—there were people bathing as others nearby washed cooking pots and bowls in the shallows, some tending small open fires, and porters ferried all manner of things up the banks from long, low boats.

Back at home, I had been a very curious child—once I'd become old enough to be allowed away from the house on my own, I'd never liked to stay in one place much. I was always keen to see what was around the next corner, which was why I'd been so eager to start living the life of my brothers, on the move and independent, and why I'd quickly chosen to leave the house with Guddu that night. But being lost in the big train station in this unsettlingly huge city had stifled that instinct—I ached for the familiar streets of home. It had made me think better of straying too far from the small area I already knew. I was torn between going back to the station and the close, confusing streets, and exploring the more open but unfamiliar territory of the river-bank. There was more and more of this city as far as I could see in every direction. Exhausted from the day's trials and lack of proper food and sleep, I kept out of people's way but had no idea what to do next. I tried hanging around some of the food stalls to see if anyone might give me something to eat, but everyone shooed me away like a stray dog. Back home I was used to being chased off when I was begging, but then I had somewhere to go at night and a family to protect me. I had never felt so alone in my whole life.

Eventually, I walked along the riverbank and came upon a group of sleeping people that I recognized as holy men. I'd seen men like these back at home. They were not like Baba at his mosque. Baba wore a long white shirt and pants, like many men in my neighborhood. These men were barefoot and wore saffron robes and beads, and some of them were quite scary looking, with wild clumps of dirty long hair wound on their heads and red and white paint on their faces. They were grubby (as I was, no doubt) from living outdoors on the streets. I had been keeping away from adults as best I could, but surely no one bad would find me here, among holy people? I lay down near the men, curled up into a ball, and joined my hands to pillow my head.

Before I knew it, morning had come and I was once again alone. The holy men had left, but the sun was up and there were people walking about.

I had survived my first night on the streets of Calcutta.

3.

———

Survival

Hungry, as usual, I found that at least there were more possibilities for food along the wide river than inside the big red train station to which I'd been transported.

As the stallholders had seemed indifferent to begging children, I went along the water's edge, thinking I might find people cooking there. Daylight confirmed that this was the biggest river I'd ever seen, but it was also fouler and smellier, lined with dead animals, human excrement, and other kinds of filth. As I picked my way along its edge, I was horrified to see two dead people lying among the piles of rubbish: one with his throat cut, the other with his ears chopped off. I'd seen dead bodies before at home, but they were always treated respectfully. And I hadn't come across any just lying outside. Here no one seemed to pay any more attention to dead people than to dead animals, even if they seemed to have been violently attacked. These bodies lay in the open, under a hot sun, covered with flies and—it appeared— gnawed by rats.

The sight made me feel sick, but what struck me most power- fully was that it confirmed what I'd already begun to feel—that every day in this city was a matter of life and death. There was danger everywhere and in everyone—there were robbers and people who took children, and I assumed even killers, based on seeing these mangled bodies. It opened up all sorts of fears. Was this the world that my brothers lived in when they went away, and the reason they never let me leave the stations when I trav- eled with them? What had happened to Guddu at the train sta- tion? Where had he got to, and why hadn't he been there when I woke up? Was he somewhere like this, looking for me? And what did my family think had happened to me? Were they look- ing, or did they think I was dead, gone, lost forever? Was I? I fell to the ground and cried wrenching tears until no more tears came out. Why had this happened to me?

More than anything, I wanted to get back home to my family, to be protected and cared for. Finally I stopped crying and sat up. No one was coming for me; I was all alone. I realized that to have any hope of returning home, I would have to be as strong as I could be. Otherwise, I would disappear, or even die, here on the bank of the wide, murky river. I understood that I had to rely on myself. In that moment, at five years old, I made a conscious decision to pull myself together and do my best to survive.

I turned back toward the bridge and came to a section of the river where people were bathing, and a set of stone steps, where people were doing laundry. There was a wide stone drain next to the steps, which brought water and waste down into the river from the street. Kids were playing, splashing, and fooling about in the water, so I went over to join in. Now it strikes me—just as it strikes many visitors to India—as incredible that anyone would wash or bathe in a river that was also a sewer and mortuary, but at the time I didn't give it a second thought. It was a river—rivers were for all of those things. They were also sites of extraordinary acts of kindness, as I was to discover.

The other children seemed to accept me joining in and we played about in the water, a respite from the heat of the day. While some of the kids were very confident, leaping off the side of the steps out into the river, I wasn't. I only walked down them far enough to be up to my knees—although my brothers had tried to teach me to swim in the dammed river near our town, I hadn't caught on yet. At home, other than in the monsoon, the river was just a gentle stream to splash in. But I loved just standing in the water. And never more so than on this day—it felt wonderful to simply be a child again, playing with other kids.

Later in the afternoon, the other children went home. I stayed on the steps, not wanting the day to end. But the river was full of surprises. I hadn't noticed, but the water level must have been rising throughout the day, and when I jumped in to what had been a safe spot earlier on, I suddenly found myself in much deeper water—over my head. There was a strong current, too, which was carrying me farther from the steps. Splashing and flailing desperately, I pushed off from the river bottom and struggled back to the surface to gasp a breath of air, but the water dragged me down and out again. This time I was too far out to reach the bottom. I was drowning.

Then I heard a splash nearby and found myself wrenched upward, pulled to the surface and onto the steps, where I sat spluttering and coughing up murky water. I had been saved by an old man who had jumped in off the stone drain just in time to pluck me from the water. Then he silently made his way back up the steps. His clothes were filthy and his teeth were red from chewing betel nut, so I supposed he lived there on the riverbank.

Perhaps the kindness of that stranger lowered my guard, or perhaps I was just too young to know better, but when I went back to swim in the river the next day, I foolishly let the rising tide and strong current surprise me again, and once more got into trouble. Amazingly, the same man rescued me—perhaps he'd kept an eye out when he saw me come back.

This time, other people noticed what had happened, seeing the man helping me up onto the steps, where I hacked up more water. A crowd formed around us, and I understood enough to realize they were declaring that the gods had spared me, that it had not yet been my time to die.

Maybe I felt overwhelmed by all the people pushing up close to stare at me, or just humiliated or annoyed with myself for having almost drowned a second time, but I leaped to my feet and ran away as fast as I could. I went far along the bank until I couldn't run anymore, vowing to keep out of the river.

I don't think I ever thanked the homeless man, my guardian angel, really, for rescuing me not once but twice.

To escape the crowd, I had run away from the area I had come to know, and night was falling. It was too late to try to get back to my part of the riverbank before dark, so I had to quickly find a new place to sleep. I came upon what looked like a disused factory, with a large pile of rubbish in the shadows at the back. Exhausted, I found a piece of cardboard and lay down on it behind the rubbish heap. The place had a bad smell, but I was becoming used to that by now, and at least it was out of sight from passersby.

That night, I was awakened by a pack of scary-looking mangy dogs barking under a nearby streetlight. I kept a rock in my hand and a pile of others within easy reach in order to scare them away if they came any closer. I must have fallen asleep like that, because when I woke with the hot sun full in my face, the rocks were still there but the dogs were nowhere to be seen.

. . .

Over the next little while, I came to know the neighborhood around the station, including the shops and stalls where I foraged for food. The smells coming from those shops were irresistible: mangoes and watermelons so ripe they were almost bursting; and from the sweets stalls, jalebis made with rosewater syrup; gulab jamuns, which were fried cheese savories served with cream; laddus, or fried sweetened dough balls; and cold lassi buttermilk. And then all I could see was people eating: a group of men cracking peanuts and chatting, some others having chai and sharing a bunch of grapes. Hunger gnawed at me then with its familiar sharp teeth, and I would go to every shopkeeper and beg desperately. They always chased me away, along with the half-dozen or so other children hanging around—there were simply too many of us to take pity on. I was so focused on just surviving day to day that I had no time to feel sorry for myself. Self-pity was a deep well that if I once fell into, I might never get out.

I'd watch people eating like a hawk—they were poor people like my family, so they didn't usually leave good food behind, but they might drop something or not finish it entirely. I would hang around waiting, my feet so tired that I would juggle between two legs, standing on one at a time to give my other foot a rest. There were no bins, so when a person was done with something, he simply threw it on the ground. I worked out what leftovers could be safely eaten, just as back at home my brothers and I knew which food to scavenge on a railway platform. Bits of fried food, like a samosa, were pretty safe once you scraped off the dirt, but they were highly prized. If a samosa was to fall to the ground, the race would be on to snatch up the remains before the other scavenging kids. Mostly I relied on things more easily spilled, like nuts or a spicy bhuja mix with dried chickpeas and lentils. Sometimes I'd race for a bit of flat bread. There were struggles among those equally desperate for scraps, and occasionally I found myself roughly shoved aside or even punched. Children didn't come out with pretty faces in the aftermath of such a skirmish; we were like wild dogs fighting over a bone.

Although I stayed mostly near the station and the river to sleep, I began to explore a few of the surrounding streets. It might have been a return of my natural wandering inclinations, but my explorations were also driven by the hunger that was my constant unwanted companion. I hoped that around that next corner might be something to eat, some source of food that the other street kids hadn't found, a kindly stallholder or a box of rejects from the market. A place this big was full of possibilities.

It was also full of trouble.

On one expedition I remember finding myself in a dense couple of blocks of tumbledown houses and shacks put together with bamboo and rusty corrugated iron. The smell was truly vile, as if something had died. I became aware of people looking at me strangely, as if I had no right to be around there, and encountered a group of older boys smoking leaf-wrapped cigarettes. I was starting to feel unnerved and stopped in my tracks as more of them began to look at me.

One boy, waving his cigarette around in his hand, stood up and approached, talking loudly in a language I couldn't understand. His friends chortled. I stood there, wondering what to do. Then he strode straight up to me and slapped my face, twice, while he kept on talking at me. Dumbfounded, I started to cry, and he hit me again, hard. I dropped to the ground and wept while the boys laughed even more.

I realized things could become worse and that I had to get out of there, so I tried to collect myself. I stood up, turned around, and started walking away at a steady pace, as you might do from a dangerous dog, my face stinging. Maybe if I showed that I didn't want to invade their turf, they would leave me alone. But when they began to come after me, I broke into a run. Through the tears in my eyes I made out a narrow gap between two buildings and darted toward it, just as I felt a rock that one of them had thrown sting my arm.

I wriggled through the gap and emerged into an enclosed yard. I couldn't see any way out, and the boys were shouting on the other side. The ground was a sea of garbage, which washed high up the far wall—perhaps I could climb it and get out that way. As I picked my way across the yard, the gang appeared through another entrance I hadn't seen. They started grabbing things out of a rusty bin, and their leader shouted at me. Then the first bottle sailed through the air and smashed against the wall behind me. More bottles followed, exploding around me—it was only a matter of time until someone got their aim right and hit me. Stumbling and ducking, I reached the rubbish heap and mercifully it held my weight. I climbed all the way up, hauled myself on top of the wall, and ran along it, praying the boys wouldn't follow me. Bottles kept smashing on the wall below and whizzing past my legs.

Maybe seeing me run was sport enough for the gang. They'd chased me off their territory and didn't bother to follow me as I wobbled along as fast as I could. A little farther on I found a bamboo ladder leaning against the wall in someone's backyard. I climbed down it and charged through the house and out the front door, past a woman sitting with her baby. She didn't even seem to notice me run by, preoccupied as she was with her infant. I headed as fast as I could back toward the bridge looming in the distance.

On the river, I was always on the lookout for a safe place to rest, as well as searching for food. Often when I returned to somewhere I'd slept before, there'd be others already there, so I moved on. Other times, I'd just come across a better prospect. Sleeping rough and the constant stress of being on the lookout meant I was always tired. Picking along the riverbank one twilight, I found myself heading under the bridge's huge structure for the first time. Beneath it, I came across a few small wooden platforms gathered together, with offerings like coconut pieces and coins, along with pictures and little statues of a goddess I recognized—Durga, the warrior form of the supreme goddess Mahadevi.

She was seated on a tiger, with her many arms whirling weapons, which in the stories I'd been told she had used to slay a demon. She was a fierce vision to behold, lit by flickering terracotta lamps. But there was also something comforting about the little lights winking in the gathering darkness all around me, and I sat there under the bridge, looking out over the river. Ever hungry, I found the offerings too tempting—I collected some of the bits of fruit and coconut, and ate them. I also took some coins.

For the first time, I felt relatively safe. I didn't want to leave this place. Along with the shrines, there were some planks set as a platform to hang out over the water. I checked that its boards were stout and stable, and clambered onto it. It felt as if I was in a sacred place, where people came to pray to the goddess. On the hard wooden planks, listening to the sound of the river flowing by beneath me, I thought about my family, wondering how they were and how they must be thinking the same thing about me.

But as I recall it, the feelings I had were different by this point than when I'd first arrived—less sharp, less painful, but somehow deeper, too. Even if home was the same, I was different. I still wanted to get back there, desperately, but the feeling didn't completely swamp me. I hadn't given up hope of returning to my family, but I had become more focused on survival, on getting through the days. I suppose I was more aware of living here than of living at a home I couldn't find. That home—the home I'd lost—felt farther away with each bit of food that I foraged, with each night I slept out in the open. Maybe I had come to feel to some degree that *this* was my home now, at least for the time being.

When I woke up the next morning, one of the wild-looking holy men in saffron robes was meditating nearby. Soon others arrived and joined him, some stripped to the waist and some carrying long, decorated walking sticks. I left quietly. I knew that I had slept in their place and taken some of their offerings, and that maybe they intended the boards over the water to be another little shrine to Durga. But they hadn't harmed me, or even woken me, and in that moment I felt secure in their company, almost as if we were on parallel journeys.

Some days, with little else to do, I would go back to the rail yards and wander among the many lines of track. There were always others about, looking for whatever they could find or else just filling up their days, like I was. Maybe they were lost, too, wondering which track might lead them home. Occasionally, a train would go by, sounding its horn to warn people out of its way.

One quiet but very hot day, I walked around until I was dazed from the heat, then sat down on a track, nearly falling asleep. A man dressed in a grimy white shirt and trousers came over.

"What are you doing hanging around such a dangerous place?" he asked.

"I'm lost," I answered in my halting way.

He replied more slowly and carefully so I could understand him. "Children are hit by trains and killed here, and others have lost arms and legs. Train stations and railway yards are dangerous. They aren't meant to be playgrounds for children."

Encouraged by the fact that he seemed to be patient enough to listen and work out what I was saying, I said, "I don't know how to get back home. I'm all alone here."

After listening to my story—the first time I'd been able to properly tell it to anyone—he told me he would take me to his home and give me food and water and a place to sleep. I was overjoyed; at last someone had stopped to help and was going to save me. I didn't hesitate to go with him.

He was a railway worker and lived in a little shack by the side of the tracks near the point at which they all converged at the entrance to the immense red station. The shack was made of corrugated iron sheets patched with some panels of thick cardboard, and was kept up by a wooden frame. He shared it with a group of other railway workers, and I was invited to join them all for dinner.

For the first time since I had become lost, I sat at a table and ate a meal that someone had cooked and that was still warm—I can still practically taste the lentil dal with rice that one of the workers made over a little fire in a corner of the shack. The workers didn't seem to mind that I was there, and didn't complain about having to share their dinner. They were very poor, but they had just enough to live by different laws than people on the streets. They had a roof, and enough for a plain meal, and a job, however hard it was. They could only offer me a tiny amount, but their willingness to feed and house a stranger made all the difference. It was like crossing into an entirely different world from the one I'd been living in, and all it took to make it was a few sheets of corrugated iron and a handful of lentils. For the second time, it felt like the kindness of a stranger had saved my life.

There was a simple spare bed in the back of the shack made out of straw, and I slept there almost as comfortably and happily as if I was in my own bed. The railway worker had mentioned that he knew someone who might be able to help me, and that he had arranged for this man to visit. I was overwhelmed with relief—already it seemed like the whole experience was a bad dream. Soon I would be home. I spent the day in the shack after the men headed off to work, waiting for my savior.

As promised, the next day another man turned up, and he also spoke carefully in plain terms that I understood. He was well dressed in a neat suit, and he laughed when I pointed at his distinctive mustache and said, "Kapil Dev," referring to India's cricket captain at the time, whom he looked like. He sat down on my bed and said, "Come over here and tell me where you are from." So I did as he asked and told him what had happened to me. He wanted to know as much as possible about where I was from so that he could help me find the place, and as I tried my best to explain everything, he lay down on the bed and had me lie down beside him.

Many lucky and unlucky things happened to me on my journey, and I made good and bad decisions. My instincts weren't always sound, but they had been sharpened by weeks of living on the streets, making conscious and unconscious decisions based on a perceived cost-benefit analysis. When we survive, we learn to trust our instincts. Perhaps any five-year-old would have begun to feel uneasy lying beside a strange man on a bed. Nothing untoward happened, and the man didn't lay a hand on me, but despite the marvelous, intoxicating promises I was being made about finding my home, I knew something wasn't right. I also knew that I shouldn't show him that I didn't trust him, that

I should play along instead. While he was saying that the next day we would go together to a place he knew and try to get me back home, I nodded and agreed. At the same time, I knew beyond question that I should have nothing to do with this man, and that I had to make a plan to get away.

That night after dinner, I washed the dishes in a worn old tub in the corner near the door, as I'd done the previous two nights. The men went into their usual huddle for their chai and a smoke, and were soon completely distracted by their conversation and jokes. This was my chance. I picked the best moment I could and bolted out the door. I ran as if my life depended on it, which in retrospect I fear it did. I hoped that by taking them by surprise, I'd get enough of a head start to escape pursuit. Once more I was fleeing into the night past the railway tracks and down streets I did not know, with no idea where to go, no thought but escape.

I was quickly exhausted and slowed down once I was in crowded streets—maybe they wouldn't even care that I was gone, and even if they did, surely they couldn't have followed me this far. Then I heard someone call out my name from quite close behind. That sent a jolt through my body like an electric shock. Immediately, I ducked down, although I was already much shorter than the people all around me, and headed for the most crowded parts of the narrow street, near the bustling stalls hawking food along the curb. When I looked around, I could glimpse

a couple of men who looked like they might be following me—
grim, hard-faced men looking around and moving fast. Then I
realized one of them was the railway worker I'd first met, who no
longer looked much like the kind man who'd taken me in. I hurried away from them, but the street soon became so crowded it
was hard to move fast, and I felt that the men were getting closer.
I had to hide. I found a small gap between two houses and ducked
into it, crawling back as far as I could before I came to a leaking
sewage pipe large enough for me to hide in. I backed into it on all
fours until I couldn't be seen from the street, ignoring the cob-
webs and the foul-smelling water running over my hands. I was
much more scared of what was out there than I was of the dark
pipe. If they found me, there was no way out.

I heard one of them talking to the fruit juice seller whose
stand was near where I was hidden. I even have a frightening
memory of peering out just as the railway worker himself looked
into the gap toward the pipe, searching with hard eyes that
seemed for a moment to stop on me but after a hesitation moved
on. Did I really come that close to being discovered? Was it the
man who had taken me in that I saw? I can't be sure now, but the
scene has remained with me as such a vivid image, perhaps
because of the power of the betrayal—I had trusted this man
and believed that he was going to help me, only for the ground
to open up beneath me and try to swallow me up. I've never forgotten that terrifying feeling.

I stayed hidden for some time, until I was certain he and the others had left, then slipped out and made my way through the darkest of the alleys and streets. I was heartbroken that all my hopes had come to nothing. The man that I'd trusted, who I thought felt sorry for me and would help me, had betrayed me. More than ever, I wished Guddu were there to protect me; he wouldn't have let anyone hurt me. I was too young to know what the man might have done to me if he'd caught me, but I knew it was a fate I wanted to avoid, and I was extremely relieved to have escaped. At least my survival instincts seemed to be strong; even if I'd made a mistake initially by trusting the man, I did know enough to run away when things took a bad turn. At some level, I took strength from the sense that I was learning to look after myself.

4.

———

Salvation

I was so scared of being found again by the railway worker and the other men that I didn't dare remain near the railway station. Despite my occasional forays into the nearby neighborhood, until then I had been too cautious to travel far from the point at which I had first arrived in the city. But now I had to. I decided to cross the river for the first time.

The walkways on either side of the long bridge were as crowded as the platforms at the station, but with many different types of people. Most were hurrying to and fro by themselves or in groups, looking very busy, but some were just hanging around as though they lived there above the water. I had to dodge families shuffling along in knots and people ferrying enormous piles of goods on their heads. I passed beggars missing limbs or eyes, some with faces ravaged and eaten away by one thing or another, all with their metal begging bowls, calling for a rupee or some food. The road in the middle was crawling with traffic of all kinds, including rickshaws and bullock carts, and even stray cows wandering through the fray. The scale of it all overwhelmed me. I pushed through as best I could and got off the main road as soon as I was on the other side.

Now, in quieter surroundings, I aimlessly wandered a maze of alleys and streets, keeping watch for both trouble and help. The railway worker had made it harder to tell the difference. Although being tricked had taught me a lesson, maybe it had also taught me that I couldn't survive on my own for very long—the dangers were too great and too hard to see. My suspicion of people had been reinforced but so had my need to find that rare person who could genuinely help me, like the homeless man by the river. I wanted to stay away from people but also find a way out of where I was. That meant I needed to keep extremely alert going forward. I had to be wary—I was terrified of falling into the hands of someone like the railway worker again—but I also had to take an occasional chance if I felt someone could help me. I mustered up the courage to approach people a little more. At some point, walking along one of the streets of my new neighborhood, I came across a boy about the same age as me talking aloud to himself, or to the world at large. When he saw me watching him, he said hello and we shyly talked for a bit. He knew more Hindi words than me and how to speak more like an adult, so he probably went to school, but he was friendly and we played around on the street for a while. Then he said I could go with him to his house. Cautiously, I followed.

When we got to his house, which was made of rusted tin and cardboard, he introduced me to his mother. Haltingly I told them a little bit of what had happened to me. The mother said that I could share a meal with them and maybe stay with them until they could find someone who might be able to get me home. My wariness slipped away in the face of what seemed to be genuine concern. I couldn't imagine this friendly woman meaning me any harm, and here was a chance to get off the streets. Even that short time in the railway worker's house had broken the habits of sleeping rough—now I wanted the safety of being inside more often, not less. I felt very happy that I was in a home, fed and sheltered.

The next day the boy's mother said I could go out with her and her son, and we walked to a nearby pond, where the locals did their laundry. She set about washing their clothes there, and the boy and I washed ourselves, too. I had worn the same black shorts and short-sleeved white shirt since I'd become lost, and I must have been very dirty. I loved being in water where I didn't need to be able to swim, and as usual could have stayed in there forever. But as the day wore on and she finished her laundry, my new friend got out and was dried and dressed. His mother started to call for me to join them. Perhaps having forgotten the ways of families and the respect expected for a mother's authority, I kept splashing about, not wanting to leave. The mother quickly lost her temper and flung a rock that missed me by a whisker. I started crying; the mother took her son, turned, and left.

I don't remember exactly what I felt, standing there in the shallows of that pond. Maybe I had misunderstood? Maybe by staying in the water, I had made them think I didn't want to join them? My mother would never have thrown a rock at me, even if she thought I was misbehaving. But the ease with which the woman had turned her back on me was the same as the ease with which she had welcomed me into her house. Was this just how people were in the big city?

Although they had left me on my own again, meeting them had still been a positive experience; as well as being given another proper meal and a place indoors to sleep, I had discovered that there were perhaps more people than I'd first thought who could be made to understand what I was saying. And, not long afterward, I found another.

One day I was hanging around near a shop front, seeing if there was a chance to scavenge some food, when a boy about the age of my brother Guddu came along, carrying goods on a hand-cart. I have no idea what made him notice me, but he said something to me that I didn't understand. He wasn't aggressive at all, so I didn't panic; I just stood and looked at him as he walked over. Then he spoke more deliberately, asking me what I was doing and what my name was.

We talked for a bit and I admitted I was lost, and he invited me to stay with his family. I might have hesitated, wondering whether he meant me harm or would turn on me, as the little boy's mother had, but I went with him. It was a risk, but so was staying on the streets. And that subconscious calculator of risk— instinct—told me that this boy meant well.

My instincts were right. He was very friendly, and I stayed at his family home for several days. Sometimes I went out with him and helped with his work hefting goods on and off his cart, and he was patient and seemed to be looking out for me. I soon learned that he was doing much more for me than that.

He began talking with me in what seemed like a different way: more adult, more serious. He told me that he was taking me to a place where I might be able to get help. We went across town together. He took me to a large police station, with many officers. Immediately, I began to resist. Was this a trick? Was he having me arrested? The teenager calmed me down, promising that the policemen didn't mean any harm, that they would try to find my home and family. I didn't really understand what was going on, but I went inside with him. The teenager spoke to the police for some time, and eventually returned to say that he was going to leave me in their care. I didn't want him to go, and I was still very nervous about the police, but my trust in this boy was strong enough to allow me to stay. I didn't know what else I could do. I was sad and scared when he said good-bye, but he said he'd done all he could and that this was the best way for me to find my way home. I hope that I thanked him.

Soon after the teenager left, I was taken out the back of the station to the lockup, where I was put in a cell with a locked door. I had no idea if things were taking a turn for the better or the worse. I didn't know it then, but in fact, as literally as the homeless man by the river had, the teenager had saved my life.

Sometimes I wonder what would have happened to me had he not taken me in or had I refused to trust him. It's possible that someone else would have done the same thing he did eventually, or that I would have been collected by some organization for homeless kids. But it's more likely I would have died on the street. Today there are perhaps a hundred thousand homeless kids in Kolkata, and a good many of them die before they reach adulthood.

Of course, I can't be sure what the railway worker's friend had planned or what happened to the children who were grabbed from the station that night I slept nearby, but I feel pretty certain that they faced greater horrors than I ever did. No one knows how many Indian children have been trafficked into the sex trade or slavery, or even for organs, but all these trades are thriving, with too few officials and too many kids.

It was only a couple of years after I was taken off the streets that the notorious "Stoneman" murders began in Calcutta, following the same phenomenon in Bombay. Somebody started murdering homeless people bedded down at night, especially around the city's major station, by dropping a large rock or slab of concrete onto their heads as they slept. Thirteen people died over a six-month period and no one was ever charged, though the killings stopped after the police detained a psychologically disturbed suspect. Had I stayed on the street, there's every chance I wouldn't be alive today.

Despite having so many memories that I wish I could forget, there are some that I wish I could remember. Among them is the name of that teenager who helped me.

I slept that night in the police lockup. The next morning, some policemen came and reassured me that I wasn't under arrest or in trouble and that they were going to try to help. I didn't feel at all comfortable with the situation, but I went along with what they said. It was my first step on the journey that took me halfway around the world.

I was given a boiled egg, rice, and dal to eat, which tasted absolutely wonderful. I gulped down every single speck of the food, down to the last grain of rice. Then I was put into a big paddy wagon with other children, both older and younger than me. We were driven through town to a building where some official-looking people gave us lunch and a drink. They asked me lots of questions, and although I didn't always understand them, it was clear that they wanted to know who I was and where I had come from. I told them what I could. They recorded my answers on their many forms and documents. "Ginestlay" meant nothing to them. I struggled to remember the name of the place where I'd boarded the train, but could only say that my brothers called it something like "Burampour," "Birampur," "Berampur . . ."

Although they took notes, they didn't really have a hope of finding these half-remembered names of comparatively tiny places that could be anywhere in the country. I didn't even know my full name; I was just "Saroo." In the end, without knowing who I was or where I'd come from, they declared my status as "Lost."

After they finished their questioning, I was taken in another van to another building, a home that they said was for children like me who had nowhere else to go. We pulled up outside a massive rusted iron door, like a prison gate, with a tiny doorway in the wall next to it. I wondered whether if I went in there I would ever come out. But I'd come this far and I didn't want to go back to the streets.

Inside there was a compound of large buildings called "the home." The one I was taken to was immense—two stories with hundreds, maybe thousands, of children playing or sitting in groups. I was taken into a huge hall with rows and rows of bunk beds stretching its length. Way down at the end of the hall, there was a communal bathroom, which was filthy.

I was shown to a bunk bed with a mosquito net, which I would be sharing with a little girl, and given food and drink. At first the home seemed how I had imagined school to be, but this school had rooms with beds, and you lived there, as in a hospital or even a prison. Certainly, over time it felt more like a prison than a school, but initially I was happy to be there, sheltered and fed.

I soon learned that there was a second hall above mine with just as many bunks, also filled with kids. Often we slept three or four to a bed, and were sometimes moved around so we ended up sharing with different people, or sleeping on the floor if it got too crowded. Children talked or shouted in their sleep, and no one rested well. The whole place was eerie, especially at night, when it was all too easy to imagine ghosts hiding in every corner.

I wonder now whether the feel of the place was somehow connected with what many of the children had been through. Some had been abandoned by their families, while others had been hurt by them and taken away. I started to feel like I was one of the luckier ones. I was malnourished but not sickly, whereas I saw children with no legs or no arms, and some with no limbs at all. There were others with awful injuries and some who could not, or would not, speak. I'd seen people with abnormalities before, and disturbed people yelling out to no one or acting crazily, especially on the streets around the station. But I could always avoid them if something about them scared me. In the home, I couldn't get away—I was living with kids with all manner of problems, including criminal and violent children who were too young to be jailed. Some were almost adults.

I later learned that this was a juvenile detention center, called Liluah, housing problem children of any and all kinds, including lost children but also the mentally ill and thieves, murderers and gang members. But back then I just knew it as a distressing place, where I would wake in the night to someone screaming or lots of frightened kids crying. What would become of me here? How long was I going to live in this horrible place?

Again I had to learn how to survive. Just as I had been picked on by boys outside, from the outset I was picked on by older boys in the home. Not having much vocabulary made me vulnerable, and my being small and relatively defenseless brought out the bully and the brute in them. Bigger boys would start taunting and making fun of me, and then push me, and if I didn't manage to get away, I was bashed. I quickly learned to stay away from certain areas when it was playtime. The staff didn't seem willing to intervene, but when they did, punishment would be meted out without regard for who was to blame: a long, thin cane was fetched, which hurt doubly, because a split end pinched the skin on contact.

There were other dangers, too, which I avoided more by luck

than by anything I planned. Liluah was surrounded by high walls, but I have memories of seeing people climb over them from the outside and enter the buildings. I never saw or heard what they did, but kids ran out crying before the strangers escaped. I don't know if the staff didn't care or were powerless to protect us, but it was a large place and I guess it was well-known as a children's home. The types of people who had tried to capture me when I was on the streets clearly didn't let walls and gates stop them. It's another thing that could have happened to me that I've tried not to think too hard about, but it's difficult not to feel upset for those who weren't so lucky. That feeling has increased as I've become older, maybe as I've learned more about the world and more about my own great good fortune. I know now that few are taken off the streets, and many of those who are have a lot of suffering ahead of them.

In the few weeks that I was at the Liluah home, some kids left through the little door in the wall, but I was never really sure why they were allowed to go or where they would be going. Maybe someone had found their families? I wondered what happened to the older ones who grew into adults within the walls. Perhaps they were sent to a different place, or just released onto the streets at a certain age.

I prayed that for whatever reason, I would be one of those who got to leave before that.

And eventually I was. Although I didn't know the reason at

the time, about a month after my arrival—because no one had reported me missing and they didn't know where I was from—the authorities decided to hand me over to an orphanage. All I knew was that I was called into the main office and told I was being taken to another home, a much nicer one. I was sent off to shower and was provided with new clothes. As always, I did as I was told. They said I was very lucky. And although they didn't seem to have found my family, I did indeed feel very lucky to be leaving what I'd come to think of as a hellish place.

Mrs. Sood, of the Indian Society for Sponsorship and Adoption (ISSA), was to become a major figure in my life. The first time I met Saroj Sood was at the children's court in Calcutta, where the Indian government released me into her custody. She had a soft, rounded face, and she exuded the sense that no harm would come to you while you were in her care. After the court session ended, she took my hand as a mother would and slowly walked me to a car that was waiting outside. Just feeling my hand held tightly in hers gave me the sense that I was safe with her.

Mrs. Sood explained that the authorities had no idea who I was or where my home and family were. She said she was going to try to find them in places that might be the "Berampur" I had talked about. In the meantime, I would get to live in her orphanage, called Nava Jeevan.

"Would you like something to eat?" she asked in her soft voice as the car started down the street.

"Kala," I said. A banana.

She smiled and had the driver stop to get me a banana, which was what I was longing for, as I hadn't had any fresh fruit in a long time. Then we continued on to my new home.

Nava Jeevan—which I've since learned is Hindi for "new life"—did turn out to be much nicer than the Liluah juvenile home, and was populated mostly by little children like me. It was a blue three-story concrete building that was also far more welcoming than Liluah. As Mrs. Sood and I walked in, I saw a few other kids peering around a corner to see the new arrival— they smiled and ran off when a woman who appeared to be in charge shooed them away. I could see into a few rooms as we walked by, where the sun streamed in on the bunk beds, which were fewer in number than those in the long halls at the home. The windows had bars, but I was beginning to understand that these were for keeping us safe rather than imprisoned. The presence of colorful posters on the walls also made it seem like a much friendlier environment than where I'd come from.

Although there seemed to be fewer children living there than in the home, it was still sometimes overcrowded at night, forcing some kids to sleep on the floor. That meant you might wake up damp from someone else's pee. In the mornings, we had a quick wash with water pumped from a well near the building's entrance and brushed our teeth using our fingers as a toothbrush. We were given a glass of hot milk with sweet Indian bread or a few milk biscuits.

It was usually quiet during the day, when many of the others went off to school. Because I had never been, I was left behind. I spent a lot of time hanging around alone on the front porch, which was enclosed with bars, like a cage. I liked our view of the large pond across the street. After a while, I got to know a girl about Guddu's age who lived on the other side of the pond, and she said hello to me as she walked past. I don't recall her name, but she seemed beautiful to me, like an actress from a movie. Occasionally, she'd pass me a snack between the bars, and one day she gave me a necklace with a pendant of the elephant-headed god Ganesh. I was astonished. It was the first present I'd ever received from anyone. I kept the necklace hidden from the other children, occasionally taking it out to gaze at in wonder. I later learned that Ganesh is often called the Remover of Obstacles, and Lord of Beginnings. I wonder whether that was why the girl chose to give it to me. (Ganesh is also Patron of Letters, and so in a way is the patron of this book.)

The necklace was more than just a beautiful object to call my own; for me, it was a concrete demonstration that there were good people in the world who were trying to help me. I still have the necklace, and it's one of my most treasured possessions.

Like there had been at the home, there were bullies at the

orphanage, although they were closer to my own age and I was able to keep clear of them. I generally stayed out of trouble, but one girl decided to run away. She had arrived after I did and was older than me. For some reason, she decided that I should go with her. I'd never thought to try to run away, but I was intimidated by her. She grabbed my hands and swept me up in her plan, and we fled through the doors together one morning before I knew what was happening. Once we were outside, I was terrified. She pulled me along as far as a sweets stall a little way down the street, where the vendor gave us each a treat to slow us down while he alerted the Nava Jeevan staff to our whereabouts. I was relieved to be back, and I don't remember being punished in any way. In fact, no one was ever hit at the orphanage, let alone caned, though you might get a dressing-down or be made to sit alone for a spell for misbehaving.

It wasn't long before Mrs. Sood told me that, despite their efforts, they hadn't managed to find my home or my family. "We haven't been able to find your mother in 'Berampur,' Saroo," she said in her friendly way. "I'm afraid there isn't anything more that we can do. But we're going to try to find another family for you to live with." As I struggled to make sense of what she was saying, I began to see the hard truth: she was telling me I would never be going home.

A part of me had already accepted this. That initial disbe-
lieving desperation to get home—that feeling that I couldn't
survive unless the world was immediately put back the way it
had been before I got lost—had long faded. The world was now
what I saw around me, the situation I was in. Perhaps I had
learned some of the lessons my brothers had learned when they
started living on their wits away from home, although I was
younger and didn't have the safety net of our mother being on
hand. I'd concentrated on what I needed to do to survive, and
that involved what was in front of me, not far away. Although I
wondered why the adults couldn't just find the right train to take
me back to where I came from and was sad at Mrs. Sood's news,
I don't remember being truly devastated by it, despite its finality.

Mrs. Sood told me that families from other countries were
happy to have lost Indian children live with them, and she
thought she could find a new family for me, if I wanted that. I'm
not sure I really understood the proposition, and I didn't give it
too much thought.

But after only four weeks in Nava Jeevan, I was taken to the
ISSA office, where Mrs. Sood told me a mother and father had
been found who wanted to take me into their home. They lived in
another country—Australia. She said it was a country that India
played at cricket, and I was aware of having heard that before, but
I knew no more about Australia. Mrs. Sood said that two boys I
knew who had recently left—Abdul and Musa—had gone there,

and a friend I had made—Asra—had also been chosen to go there. Australia was a good place that was helping poor children without families and giving them opportunities most children in India would never have.

Back at Nava Jeevan, Asra and I were each shown bewitching little red photograph albums that the people offering to become our new families had made. Inside were pictures of them, their houses, and other aspects of their lives. I looked through mine with my eyes popping out of my head. The people looked so different from what I was used to—for one thing, they were white! And everything around them looked shiny, clean, and new. The book was even addressed to me: "Dear Saroo."

"Look at this!" I said to Asra, pointing to a photo of a man washing a car.

The staff worker read the English caption to me: "This is your father washing our car, in which we will visit many places." I couldn't believe it; my new parents had a car!

"This is the house that will be our home," the worker continued reading. It was very grand, with lots of glass windows, and it looked brand-new. "The family is called Mr. and Mrs. Brierley," she added.

There was also a picture of a jet plane ("This plane will bring you to Australia"), which fascinated me. Back at home, I had seen jets flying high up in the sky, leaving their vapor trails streaking behind them, and had always wondered what it would be like to sit in a plane up in the clouds. If I agreed to go to these people, I would find out.

Getting used to the idea of living with a new family in a foreign land was an overwhelming experience. Asra was very excited and often asked for us to again be shown our books, which were held by the staff for safekeeping. She would sit down with me and open hers, point to a picture, and say, "This is my new mum" or "This is my new house." I would join in: "This is *my* new house! This is *my* new dad's car!" We encouraged each other, and her enthusiasm rubbed off on me. It was a little like having a storybook all about me, even though I wasn't in it. It was hard to believe it was real. All I knew about Australia was in that red book, but I really couldn't have thought of anything else to ask.

At Nava Jeevan everyone cried from time to time about the parents they had lost. Some children's parents had abandoned them, and other parents had died. I was the only one who simply didn't know where my family was, and no one could help me find them. But we had all lost our families in one way or another, and there was no going back from that. Now I was being offered a chance to join a new family.

Asra was already talking about her new family with joy and excitement. I don't know that I was truly given a choice, and I'm sure some gentle persuasion would have been brought to bear had I expressed doubts about Australia or Mr. and Mrs. Brierley. But it wasn't necessary. I knew there wasn't much I could do if I didn't accept this opportunity. Would I go back to the home where I was bullied? Go back to the streets and keep taking my chances? Keep searching for a train not even the adults could find?

I told the folks at the orphanage that I wanted to go to Australia.

When I agreed to join the new family, it made everyone so happy that the mood was infectious: immediately, any last reservations melted away. I was told that I'd be going to Australia very soon to meet my new parents and on a jet plane just like the one in the picture.

Asra and I were about the same age, but the others going to Australia were only toddlers or babies. I don't know if that made what was happening more or less scary for the littler ones—how much did they understand? I was both excited and terrified, but at least Asra was coming, too, so there would be one familiar face on the trip. And the pictures in the photograph album were so enticing that our fears were calmed somewhat.

One day we were washed and dressed nicely, and some of the boys and girls were taken for a drive in separate taxis. The boys went to the house of a woman we were told to call Aunty Ula. She was a white woman from Sweden, although of course that meant nothing to me, but she welcomed us in Hindi. Her house was better than anything I'd ever seen, with rich-looking furniture, curtains, and carpet—something like the photos in my red book. We sat at a dining table and I was presented for the first time with a knife and fork and taught how to use them correctly—I'd only ever eaten with my hands before.

"Now, you don't just get up and reach for things," Aunty Ula said in a kind way. "We must ask for things properly and sit up straight."

Obediently we all straightened in our seats.

"Say, 'Please, may I have more rice,'" she instructed, and we repeated after her. Just the thought of being able to ask for more food with the expectation of receiving it made me happy and built up my excitement to an almost unbearable pitch. It seemed that we were about to embark on the adventure of our lives.

We didn't receive any lessons in English, although at Nava Jeevan there was a pictorial alphabet wall chart with "A is for Apple" and so on. I think I was taught to say "Hello," but there was no time for more than that—I was due to leave India almost immediately. I was leaving for a place I had been told was far away, at a distant end of the world. No one ever talked about my coming back, and it didn't seem to be on anyone's mind.

Everyone agreed I was very lucky.

So I left India only a few days after I was told about my adoption (only a month or so after I arrived at the orphanage—which in today's more regulated processes is pretty much unheard of—and only about six months after leaving my mother's house in "Ginestlay"). The six of us from Nava Jeevan who were flying to Australia, including my friend Asra, were joined by two more children from a different orphanage for the journey. After a stopover in Bombay (not yet known as Mumbai), we would fly first to Singapore and on to Melbourne, where our new families would meet us. Asra's new family lived in Victoria, and my new family, the Brierleys, was a second trip away, in Tasmania, the island state about 240 kilometers south of mainland Australia.

I was sad to learn that we were saying good-bye to Mrs. Sood. Three volunteer Australian women and a man from an Australian government department would escort us on the flight. They were all very friendly, and although we couldn't communicate much, the excitement of the journey was enough to obliterate any separation anxiety.

I was over the moon when I finally boarded that huge plane. It seemed impossible that such a thing with so many seats and so many people could fly, but I don't remember being worried about it, only excited. We were each given a chocolate bar, an amazing luxury to me, which I carefully made last the entire journey. We talked and watched a film with headphones on. I was fascinated by the plug in the armrest and being in control of the channel and the volume. We ate everything we were given under those little foil lids. The fact that people brought food to us already seemed like the start of a new, luxurious life. I suppose we also slept.

When we arrived in Bombay, we stayed overnight in a hotel, which brought a new round of fresh amazement. It probably wasn't any more than a regular hotel in the West, but it was the fanciest place I'd ever seen. The room smelled so fresh, and I had never slept in such a soft, clean bed. Even with the excitement of everything that was happening, I had the best sleep I'd had for months. I marveled at the bathroom, with its shiny shower and toilet. Around the hotel I saw more white people than I'd ever seen in one place, and although it's embarrassing to admit, all I remember thinking is that they looked so rich. There was so much that was new going on around me, I don't know if I thought about how I would soon be living with white people like them.

The next day I was given a new pair of white shorts and a "Tasmania" T-shirt, which had been sent by my new parents for me to wear on the plane to Australia. I was delighted with my outfit. Better still, we were taken to a toy shop nearby, where we were invited to choose a toy each—I guess there were limits on its extravagance, though I don't remember being told so. I still have the little car I chose, with its pullback mechanism that launched it across the room.

I know now that flying from Calcutta to Bombay had meant passing very close to my hometown, thirty thousand feet below. The plane I was on must have left one of those vapor trails I had watched with such fascination. I wonder if my mother unknowingly looked up at the right moment and saw my plane and its streaky trail. She would have been astonished beyond belief to know I was on board.

5.

_____

A New Life

We landed in Melbourne on the night of September 25, 1987. Our escorts led us to a VIP area of the airport, where we were told our new families would be waiting to meet us.

I felt very shy as I walked into the room. There were lots of adults, all watching us as we came in. I immediately recognized the Brierleys from the photos I had pored over in my red book. I tried to smile as I stood there, and looked down at the last bit of precious chocolate bar in my hand. (The picture on the front of this book was taken when I first walked into the room in Melbourne—you can see the chocolate in my hand.)

An escort took me across the room and the first word I said to my new parents was "Cadbury." In India, Cadbury is synonymous with chocolate. After we hugged, Mum got straight to work being a mother and produced a tissue to clean my hand.

Because I didn't speak much English, and my new mum and dad didn't speak any Hindi, we couldn't talk to each other. So we sat together and looked through the red book they'd sent me. Mum and Dad pointed out the house I would live in and the car we would use to drive there, and we began to get used to each other's company as much as we could. I suppose, too, I must have been a difficult child to reach—cautious and reserved after everything I'd been through. You can see that from my face in the pictures—not alarmed or anxious, especially, just a bit with-drawn, waiting to see what would happen. But despite all this, straightaway I knew I was safe with the Brierleys. It was just intuition—they had a quiet, kind manner, and there was a warmth in their smiles that put me at ease.

I was also calmed by seeing Asra happily interacting with her family. She eventually left the airport with them, and I suppose we said good-bye in the cursory way children do. But my family had another short flight to make, from Melbourne over Bass Strait to Hobart, the capital of Tasmania. So our first night together was spent in the airport hotel, sharing a room.

Mum put me straight into the bath, lathering me up and dous-ing me to kill nits and the like. I arrived in a very different con-dition from most kids in Australia. In addition to the external parasites, it turned out I had an intestinal tapeworm, broken teeth, and a heart murmur (which happily didn't last). Being poor in India took its toll on your health, and living on the streets wore you out even more.

I slept soundly that first night in Australia—clearly I was getting used to hotels. When I woke the next morning, I saw Mum and Dad were watching me from their bed, waiting for me to stir. At first I just looked out at them from under the sheets. Mum says she can still picture that morning clearly. She and Dad raised their heads from their double bed to peer across the room at the little mound of sheets in the single bed with a mop of black hair sticking out. And every now and then I would peep out at them. Afterward, when I was still small and we'd recall that first night as a family, I'd remind them, "I peeping, I peeping."

I don't know that any of us could quite believe it was happening—that these strangers in the room were going to be my parents, or that this boy from India was going to be their son.

After breakfast, it was back on a plane for the short flight to Hobart, where I got a first look at my new country from borders beyond the window of a hotel or airport. To eyes used to the crush and pollution of one of the most populous places on earth, it seemed so empty and so *clean*—the streets, the buildings, even the cars. There wasn't a soul to be seen as dark-colored as me, but then, there was hardly anyone to see at all. It looked almost deserted.

As we drove through the unfamiliar countryside and into Hobart's suburbs, I saw a city of gleaming palaces, including my new home. I recognized it from the red book, but it looked even bigger and more impressive in reality. Inside there were four bedrooms for only three people, each of the rooms huge and so neat. A carpeted living room, with comfortable couches and the biggest TV I'd ever seen, a bathroom with a big bath, a kitchen with shelves full of food. And a refrigerator: I loved standing in front of it just to feel the cold air come out whenever it was opened.

Best of all, though, was my bedroom. I'd never had a room to myself. Both houses I'd lived in in India were single rooms, and since then, of course, I'd been in dormitories with other children. But I don't remember being intimidated about sleeping on my own—perhaps my time sleeping on the streets had made me used to it. I was afraid of the dark, though, and required my bedroom door to be left open and a light on in the hall.

On my own soft bed, with a big map of India on the wall above it, there were new, warm clothes for the cool Tasmanian climate. I had experienced some cooler weather in India but had never had such cozy clothing. And on the floor were boxes full of picture books and toys; my favorite was my koala bear, which they gave to me on the night I arrived. It took me a little while to realize they were for me—*all* of them—and that I could look at them and play with them as I pleased. I felt cautious, maybe half expecting someone to come along and take them. The idea of *having possessions* took some getting used to. Nevertheless, for the most part adapting to the Western lifestyle seemed easy, and with Mum and Dad's guidance, I settled in well.

Another thing that took some getting used to was the abundance of things to eat. I was amazed at how big their refrigerator was. It was well stocked with plenty of colorful food, and was wonderful to look into and see all the delicious things inside. I learned the names of the various foods by helping my mum cook. We would exchange their names: my mum in English, with me naming things in Hindi, particularly the spices. She fed me things that would build my strength, and I grew very quickly.

At first we ate a lot of Indian food, which tasted a little different from what I was used to back home but was delicious all the same. In addition, Mum slowly introduced me to an Australian diet. There were some big differences, and not just in taste: Mum remembers I noticed her putting red meat into the refrigerator once and ran up to her crying, "Cow, cow!" For a child brought up a Hindu, to slaughter the holy animal was taboo. For a moment she didn't know what to do, but then she smiled and said, "No, no, it's beef." Apparently, in the end, the delight I took in having abundant food close at hand overcame most matters of taste or culture.

I loved going to the swimming pool. The first time we went, Mum got into the water while I stood on the side wearing floaties.

But I couldn't wait, so I just jumped right in. My swimming was poor, but with Mum's help and by copying other kids nearby, I picked it up quickly. We went every week, and soon I was able to swim on my own.

One aspect of life in Australia that immediately appealed to me was experiencing nature in the outdoors. In India, I was always in a town or city—often free to roam but nevertheless surrounded by buildings and roads and people. In Hobart, my parents were very active, taking me to play golf, camp, hike, and sail. Dad often took me out on his two-man catamaran, which built upon my curiosity and love for the water, and allowed me to truly improve upon my swimming skills. Just being able to look out at the horizon gave me peace of mind. India was so choked with development, you often couldn't see anything but the press of buildings around you—it was like being in a giant maze. Some people find the bustle of busy cities exciting and energizing, but you see a different side of them if you're begging or trying to make people stop and listen to you. So once I got used to Hobart, I found its open spaces reassuring.

We lived in the suburb of Tranmere, across the river from central Hobart, and after about a month I started school in the next suburb, Howrah. Only years later did I realize an incredible coincidence. A couple of months before I arrived in Australia, I'd been surviving on the streets of Calcutta in an area also named Howrah, which gives its name to the city's huge railway station and famous bridge. The Hobart version is a pretty beach-side suburb, with schools, sports clubs, and a large shopping center. It was apparently named in the 1830s by an English army officer who had served in the West Bengal capital and upon coming to live in Hobart had seen something similar in the look of the hills and the river. If there was any resemblance then, it's lost now.

I loved school. I used to say to Mum and Dad after I came home, "I'm learning like magic!" Since there is no free education in India, I probably never would have made it to school without coming to the Tasmanian Howrah. Like the rest of the community, it was quite an Anglo-Saxon place, although there were a couple of kids from other countries. I had extra English lessons with another student from India and one from China. After two months, the school year ended, and the following fall I began grade one.

Although I'd become quite used to the change of color and culture around me, I still stood out to everyone else, especially since I have white parents. Other kids talked about their families and how they came from the country or from Melbourne, and they would ask me where I was from, but all I could say was "I'm from India." But kids are curious—they wanted to know why I was here in a white family. Mum defused a lot of this by attending a parent-student day and telling the class about my adoption. It seemed to satisfy my peers, and they didn't ask much after that.

I don't remember any racism at school. Mum, however, tells me there were some things said that I didn't understand properly. Perhaps that was an advantage in having to master the local language from scratch. Apparently I once asked her, "What's a 'black basket'?" which upset her. She chose not to explain that someone had called me a "black bastard."

Another time, my dad and I were lining up to register me for a sports team. The woman in front of us glanced back and then said in a low voice to the coach, "I don't want my son on the same team as that black boy."

We just ignored it, signed up for the team roster, and left. I don't mean to make light of comments like that, but in comparison with the experiences I've heard from other non-Anglos, I don't think I had it too bad, and I've always felt that I grew up without any scars from racism.

That might not have been true for Mum and Dad. I'm told we did attract some negative attention at the local Indian Cultural Society, which conducted dinners and dances. There was quite a large Indian community in Hobart, from Fiji and South Africa as well as from India, and for a time we went along and enjoyed the society's events. But my parents came to notice that we were treated a little suspiciously, and determined that it was considered somehow wrong for an Indian child to be taken from India by white parents. Needless to say, I was oblivious to this.

Another organization we were involved in was ASIAC, the

Australian Society for Intercountry Aid (Children), which helped people adopt from overseas. Mum became very active, helping other Australian families with the constantly changing processes as well as the personal challenges. Through that organization, I met other children who'd come to Australia from elsewhere and now lived in mixed-race families. Mum tells me that at our first ASIAC picnic I seemed surprised—and perhaps a little put out—to discover I wasn't the only "special one" in Hobart. Yet I made friends, one of whom was Ravi, another Indian boy, who lived with his new family in Launceston, and our families visited each other often during those early years.

ASIAC also put me back in touch with some of the other kids from Nava Jeevan. My closest friend, Asra, had ended up with a family in the riverside Victorian town of Winchelsea, and our families had kept us in phone contact. A year after I arrived, all of us met up at a zoo in Melbourne with two other kids from the orphanage who had been adopted into Australia, Abdul and Musa. I was overjoyed to see familiar faces, and we all busily compared notes on our new lives, measuring them against our time in the orphanage together. Although it hadn't been a terrible place, I don't think any of us wished ourselves back there. We didn't talk about our past lives in India, but it seemed to me that both of them were as happy in their new homes as I was.

Later the same year Mrs. Sood herself arrived in Hobart, escorting another new adoptee, Asha, whom I remembered from the orphanage. It made me happy to see Mrs. Sood again—she'd taken good care of us, and until I left India, she was probably the most friendly and trustworthy person I had met after becoming lost. I like to think that for her part it must have been satisfying to see some of the children she'd helped in their new environments. Mrs. Sood dealt with a huge amount of trauma among her charges, but I've always thought the rewards must have been equally large. I'm sure that some adoptions don't work out as well as mine did, but I also imagine that occasional visits to the children she'd connected with new families gave her renewed energy to return to work.

I was no slouch in school, despite the fact that my English was still under development. I got on well with my teachers and loved them, and they seemed to love me, too. In my middle primary years, I did very well, even skipping a year, which coincided with a huge growth spurt. Then when I got to secondary school, the gap in my learning from that missed year became evident, and I struggled with written language for a while. Outside of school, my mum and dad continued to take me camping, sailing, and hiking. I loved the outdoors as they did, and we went on many fun holidays together. I felt safe and secure in my new life.

· · ·

When I was ten, Mum and Dad adopted a second child from India. I was keen on the idea of having a sibling. In fact, it seemed that the person I missed most from India was my sister. "What do you want for Christmas?" my mum would ask me every year. "I want Shekila back," I often said.

Of course, I missed my mother deeply, but from the first moment that I was introduced to Mum, she had done a brilliant job of being a mother to me, and having a father's attention also made me very happy. They couldn't replace my being with my birth mother, but they did lessen the loss as much as they could. The one person really absent from my life was a brother or sister—especially since I was used to being left for long periods without any parent around when I was in my home village.

In India, Shekila had been my special responsibility. She was the family member I was most closely bonded with, and most haunted by. I worried that she might be sick or hungry, that her hands and face weren't clean. I had been her guardian, and it was hard not to know what was happening to her now. Sometimes I told my mum that I felt guilty for not looking after Shekila as well as I should have. With all this on my mind, I was looking forward to having a sibling in Australia. When Mum and Dad had applied to adopt the first time, they hadn't put any gender conditions or restrictions of any kind on their application. They were happy to have whatever child needed a home; that's how they got me. So they did exactly the same thing the second time. We might have acquired a young girl, or a child older than me, but as it happened, we got my little brother, Mantosh.

I didn't care that he wasn't a sister—the idea of having another child to play with at home was enough for me. And—assuming he'd be rather quiet and shy at first, like I was—I thought I could help him adjust to this new life. He'd be someone for me to help look after.

But Mantosh and I were very different, partly because of the natural differences between people, but also because of our different experiences in India. It's one of the things that makes people who adopt children, especially from abroad, so brave: often the kids they're taking in come with troubled backgrounds, having suffered in ways that make adjusting to their new life difficult, which can be hard to understand and even harder to help. At first I was reticent and reserved; Mantosh was loud and disobedient. I wanted to please; he rebelled.

What we did have in common was that Mantosh's background had a lot of unknowns in it, too. He'd also grown up poor and with no formal education, and he can't say for sure exactly where or when he was born. He arrived as a nine-year-old with no birth certificate, medical records, or any official documentation of his origins. We celebrate his birthday on

November 30 because that's the day he landed in Australia. Like me, it was as if he simply fell to earth, but lucky for him, he landed in the care of the Brierleys in Hobart.

Mantosh's story as we now know it is this: He was born somewhere in or near Calcutta and grew up speaking Bengali. His mother fled their violent family home, leaving him behind, and he was sent to live with his frail grandmother. But she couldn't even look after herself properly, much less a little boy, so she handed him over to the state and eventually he ended up in the care of ISSA and Mrs. Sood's adoption agency, as I had. The legal process permitted orphans to live in an ISSA orphanage for two months while attempts were made to restore them to their family or arrange an adoption. Mrs. Sood was excited by the idea of placing Mantosh with the Brierleys so we would become brothers.

But Mantosh didn't enjoy the same smooth process of adoption as I had. Because he *did* have parents, even though he couldn't return to them—his mother's whereabouts were unknown and his father didn't want him—there were complications in the attempts to make him available for adoption. With his two months exhausted, he had to be transferred back to Liluah—the intimidating juvenile home I had been sent to—while ISSA continued to try to arrange his adoption by Mum and Dad. At Liluah, Mantosh wasn't as lucky as I'd been. He was physically and sexually abused. Later it emerged that in the past he'd been abused by his uncles as well.

It took two years for the complex legal procedures to be worked through, by which time he'd obviously been scarred terribly by his experiences. The only positive was that he'd learned more English than I had, which helped him when he arrived in Australia. What happened to Mantosh exposed the harm that the bureaucratic adoption system can inflict. When I learned about his past, later on, I couldn't stop thinking about the nights I'd spent in the Liluah juvenile home, and how easily I could have experienced trauma similar to what Mantosh had experienced.

When Mantosh first arrived, he didn't seem completely sure of what adoption meant—he didn't seem to understand that his move here was permanent. The situation might not have been explained to him clearly enough, or he just wasn't as certain as I had been that this was the right thing to do. When he began to understand that he wasn't going back to India, he had mixed feelings—the sort of ambivalence that's understandable in all adoptions, and which I had experienced myself, although to a much lesser extent. That was compounded by an emotional volatility doubtless caused by his traumas. When he was young, he could become explosively angry without any obvious provocation, and though he was an emaciated little boy, he could be as strong as a man. Once, I asked him to give a toy back to me, and when he wouldn't, we pushed each other around for a while. That was when I realized he was stronger than I was, despite his size. I'd never experienced anything like it, and unfortunately, it made me somewhat wary of him when we were little. Mum and Dad were patient and loving but firm, and both Mantosh and I think all the more of them for their determination to make a family out of the four of us.

Still, although I understand things now, at the time I was unsettled. Because of the difficulties that Mantosh was going through, he required most of our parents' attention. I was reasonably well-adjusted by then, but I still needed reassurance that I was loved and cared for. Sibling rivalry born out of a perceived imbalance of parental attention at home is, of course, normal, but it's easier for me to realize now that Mantosh and I both had insecurities from our pasts that probably made us react more strongly than most. As a result, I even ran away from home one night soon after Mantosh arrived. It was a measure of how much I'd changed—and how much I'd learned about the resilience and underlying love in a family—that I didn't even attempt to live on the streets again. Much more typical of a Western kid testing his parents' commitment to him, I only made it to the local bus depot around the corner. I soon got cold and hungry and went home. Although Mantosh and I had our differences, we also went swimming and fishing together, and played cricket and rode our bikes, like most young brothers.

Mantosh didn't enjoy school as much as I did. He was frustrated and disruptive in class, although he at least shared my enthusiasm for sport. Unlike me, he seemed to attract racist comments, to which he would retaliate and then find himself in trouble. That encouraged his bullies, who would make a game of stirring him up. Unfortunately, the teachers were ill-equipped to assist someone struggling to adjust to a new way of life. And it didn't help that Mantosh wasn't used to accepting direction from women in authority, a prejudice that stemmed from cultural norms in India.

I'd had to learn some of these differences, too. Mum remembers taking me somewhere in the car once when I looked at her and said, "Lady no drive." She pulled over and said, "If lady no drive, then boy walk!" I quickly learned my lesson.

I know Mum feels some regret that because Mantosh needed so much of my parents' attention, I spent more time left to my own devices than I might have otherwise. But other than throwing the occasional tantrum, I wasn't much bothered, perhaps because that's what I had been used to in India. I liked my independence. And we still did plenty of things together as a family—we would go to a restaurant every Friday as a family outing and took trips away during school holidays.

At one point, Mum and Dad planned a major family trip—to travel to India together. At first I was extremely enthusiastic about it, and Mantosh seemed to like the idea, too. We'd always been surrounded by Indian things and thought a lot about the country, so we all talked excitedly about what we'd see and where we'd go. Of course, neither of us knew where our hometowns were, so we'd visit other places and learn more about the country we were from.

But as the date of the trip neared, Mantosh and I both began to feel anxious. There was no avoiding the fact that our memories of India weren't happy ones, and the more real the prospect of going back became, the more vivid those memories seemed to be. A lot of things that we'd been able to put behind us—or at least put out of our minds—returned. I certainly didn't want to go back to Calcutta, and I began to be agitated that any other place we visited might turn out to be my home or somewhere I would recognize. I still wanted to find my other mother, but I was happy where I was—I wanted both things. It was confusing and increasingly upsetting. And maybe subconsciously I was worried about getting lost again. I can only imagine what must have been going through Mantosh's mind.

In the end, our parents decided that the trip would stir up too many emotions and it was better for the moment to let sleeping dogs lie.

6.

———

My Mum's Journey

I couldn't write about my journey without explaining how my parents came to make their choice to adopt two children from India. And not two specific children—as I've mentioned, they were prepared to give a home to whichever two children they were sent, of any gender, age, or circumstance, which was unusual for adoptive parents from the West. That seems to me a particularly remarkable and selfless act, and how they came to do it is part of my story.

My mum—Sue—was born on the northwest coast of Tasmania to parents who had emigrated from central Europe after World War II. Both of her parents had rough times growing up.

Mum's mother, Julie, was born in Hungary to a poor family

with fourteen children. Julie's father went off to work in Canada as a lumberjack, with the intention of sending back money, but he never returned, abandoning his wife and all their children. The older children tried to help out as best they could, but when the war came, most of the brothers were taken away to fight and died in battle. By the time the Russians arrived in Hungary to pursue the retreating Nazis, Julie's family had fled into Germany and didn't return. (When the fighting ended in Hungary, some of the villagers who had been displaced tried to go back to their homes, but Julie's family decided it was too dangerous. Many Hungarians who did return found Russians living in their homes, and when they tried to reclaim them, they were shot down in the streets.) Julie was just nineteen years old as the war was drawing to an end.

Mum's father, Josef, was Polish and had a traumatic childhood of his own. When he was five years old, his mother died and his father took a new wife. His stepmother hated Josef so much it's said that she tried to poison him, and he was eventually sent away to be brought up by his grandmother. Mum says that because of his stepmother, Josef's grandmother raised him with a deep bitterness against women.

When Nazi Germany invaded Poland at the start of the war, Josef joined the Resistance and took part in bombing and shooting missions but became deeply disturbed by the experience. Finally, despite his role in the Resistance, he, too, fled the advancing Russians and ended up in Germany.

Josef was a good-looking man—literally tall, dark, and hand-some—and when Julie met him, in the chaos at the tail end of the war, she fell in love. They married, and by the time the war was over, they had a baby, Mary. It was a turbulent period, with displaced people on the roads and on trains all across Europe. When the couple wanted to travel to the New World to start over, they managed to get themselves to Italy and boarded a ship they thought would take them to Canada, but it ended up sailing to Australia. So like a good number of refugees, they ended up in a place they hadn't chosen and had to make the best of it.

Julie spent at least a year in the Victorian migrant camp at Bonegilla, near Albury-Wodonga, taking care of the baby, while Josef was contracted to build houses in Tasmania and lived on his own at a work camp. The idea was that he would send for them when he had a place suitable for a family—something that must have reminded Julie of her father—but Josef was as good as his word, and when the opportunity came up to share a farm with another family outside the town of Somerset, near Burnie, Josef and Julie were reunited. Josef worked hard, and before long he bought the farm next door and built their own cottage. Mary was six when Mum was born in 1954. Sixteen months later, Mum had a younger sister, too, Christine.

Like many survivors of the war, Josef had been left psycholog-ically disturbed, which became more apparent as the years went on. Mum's early upbringing was very harsh, especially because of her father's moods, which swung between melancholia, rage, and violence. She describes him as a big, powerful, frightening man. He came from a background in which beating wives and children was commonplace.

Polish to the core, Josef drank a lot of vodka—every day—and also insisted on unvarying traditional meals of pan-fried pork with cabbage and potatoes. Mum hated it and became an emaciated and unhealthy child. She says that to this day it still makes her feel queasy to talk about what they had to eat.

Josef made a considerable amount of money through his building business and acquired a lot of property. Mum thinks he might even have been Somerset's first millionaire, although no one is sure exactly how much he was worth. Unfortunately, as his condition worsened, he became delusional and deranged, and was notorious for his bad business dealings. He also refused to pay taxes on his properties. It might have had something to do with his mental health or his refusal to recognize civic authority, but he simply would not pay up. This led to his downfall and broke up the family.

My mum grew up quickly and managed to lift herself out of her difficult circumstances. She left school in Year 10, when her father insisted she get a job, and started work in Burnie as a pharmacy assistant. Her wage gave her some independence for the first time in her life. She earned around fifteen dollars a week, two dollars of which she was proud to give her mother for her board. She used most of the rest to assemble a glory box, or hope chest, with everything she might need for the married life she hoped would come. At sixteen, after years of stress and undernourishment at home, she felt like her life had turned around at last.

One day on a lunch break with a couple of her girlfriends, Mum noticed a young man who was up "all the way" from Hobart—a visitor from the capital was news in Burnie. His name was John Brierley. He later asked the girls about their friend Sue, and not long afterward she had a phone call from him inviting her out.

John was a twenty-four-year-old handsome surfie, blond and tanned, polite and easygoing. His English father was a British Airways pilot who had retired at fifty and emigrated with his family to the warmer climate of Australia. The teenage John hadn't been too sure about leaving England at first, but once he got to Australia and into the sun-and-surf lifestyle, there was no looking back. Dad hasn't been to England since.

Mum hadn't been interested in boyfriends before she met Dad, largely because of her experiences with her father. It was only when her older sister, Mary, met her own husband-to-be

that Mum first encountered a man who was decent and respect-
ful, and who wouldn't beat his wife and children. It helped her
see that some men could be trusted.

In 1971, a year after they met, Dad was offered a position that
would require transferring to the mainland, but rather than leave
Mum behind, he stayed in Tasmania and proposed. They were
married on a Saturday and moved to a small flat in Hobart, and
Mum started work on the following Monday at a pharmacy there.
It was as if he had turned up on a white horse and swept her off
her feet; the next thing they knew, they were married and creating
a home together. With hard work and saving, they bought a block
of land in the waterside suburb of Tranmere and started building.
Mum turned twenty-one in her own home in 1975.

Though Mum managed to leave Burnie, her family's fortunes
worsened, which affected her deeply. Her father, Josef, went
bankrupt twice. The second time was for the sake of a five-
hundred-dollar tax fine he refused to pay. He was sent to the
Burnie lockup until his debts were cleared. Mum and the rest of
the family didn't know it then, but he had thousands of dollars
secretly stashed in the house that could have bailed him out had
he told them about it.

It was the beginning of a downward spiral. The accountant
appointed by the court held a fire sale to retrieve a few thousand
dollars in outstanding taxes and the fine, and then claimed more

than the revenue raised for his fee, leaving the family with its old debt and a new one to the accountant. When Mum was around thirty, Josef was hauled off to prison in Hobart, where, clearly suffering from alcohol withdrawal on top of everything else, he became excessively violent and was transferred to a psychiatric prison.

There Josef borrowed money from a loan shark who in less than a year managed to take his remaining property in interest repayments, leaving the family with nothing. Mum's mother finally left her volatile husband a year later; Josef, still in prison, threatened to kill her, blaming her for everything. She moved into a flat, where she suffered illness caused by a nearby toxic paper mill, until Mum—by this time a mother to two adopted sons—was able to bring her to join us in Hobart. Mantosh and I enjoyed having our gran close by. Though Josef had been discharged by then, Mum didn't want to expose Mantosh and me to his troubled nature, and we never met him. He died when I was twelve.

Mum's hard times made her strong-willed and determined, and gave her different priorities from the other women she knew. The early years of her marriage were a time of change in Australia: the Whitlam Government was voted in after the upheavals of the sixties, and the social and political landscape was being transformed. Even though Mum and Dad weren't exactly hippies, they were attracted to the "alternative" ideas being bandied about.

People were particularly worried about overpopulation, and there was a growing concern about the impact of so many billions of people on the world's environment. There were other issues, too, including war. Dad was fortunate not to have been sent to fight in Vietnam. Their progressive views helped Mum form the idea that one way to make a difference was to adopt children in need from developing countries.

Because of all she'd been through growing up, Mum had decided that there was nothing sacrosanct about families formed only by birth parents. Though brought up Catholic, in a culture where women were expected to bear children, she and Dad thought the world had enough children born into it already, with many millions of them in dire need. They agreed that there were other ways to create a family beyond having children themselves.

There was also an amazing personal moment in Mum's past that she says put her on the path to her nontraditional family. When she was about twelve years old, the pressures from her family's issues led her to something like a breakdown, during which she had what she can only describe as a "vision." It left her feeling like an electric shock had gone through her. The vision was of a brown-skinned child standing by her side—she sensed it so keenly that she could even feel the child's warmth. It was so striking she wondered about her sanity, and even whether it was possible she'd seen a ghost. But as time went by, she became more comfortable with her vision and came to accept it as something precious, a visitation of some sort that only she knew about. It was the first time in her bleak life that she'd experienced an overwhelming feeling of something fortuitous, and she held on to it.

As a young married adult, with a like-minded husband, she had the chance to make her vision come true. So although they were able to have children themselves, Mum and Dad agreed that they would adopt children from poor backgrounds and give them a much-needed home and loving family. Dad admits that Mum was the driving force in their decision to adopt. In fact, Mum says that she felt so strongly about it that if they hadn't agreed on it, it might have been the end of their marriage. But Dad was more than happy with their plan, and once they'd made the decision, they never wavered.

They were, though, given plenty of cause to rethink. As soon as they started making official inquiries, they hit a problem—under Tasmanian state law at the time, couples who could conceive weren't permitted to adopt. For the time being, that was simply that. They didn't change their principles; instead, they chose to sponsor children in need overseas (as they still do) and otherwise enjoy their own good fortune childlessly, dining out, sailing, and taking holidays every year.

However, adoption always remained at the back of their collective mind. There was obviously no biological clock ticking for them, and the other constraint at the time—specifying a maximum age difference of forty years between the youngest adopting parent and the child, to avoid young children being adopted by elderly people who might struggle to take care of them—was unlikely to affect them, as they hadn't requested a child of any particular age.

Sixteen years passed after their resolution to adopt. Then one day Mum met a beautiful little brown-skinned girl, Maree, who had been adopted by a local family who also had a biological son. Mum realized that meant the law preventing fertile parents from adopting must have been changed. She felt the hairs go up on the back of her neck—she had an uncanny feeling that this girl could have been the child by her side in her vision as a twelve-year-old. It prompted her to once again inquire about adoption, and to her joy she confirmed that she and Dad could now apply to adopt children from overseas. Despite having long before established the rhythms of their life, they had no hesitation about starting the process.

After many interviews, lots of document preparations, and police checks, Mum and Dad were approved to adopt. They then had to choose a country to send their file to. They had heard from an adoption group in Victoria that the agency ISSA, in Calcutta, had a humanitarian focus and acted more quickly than elsewhere to place needy Indian children in new homes. Mum had always been fascinated by India and knew something about the conditions many people were living under there: in 1987 Australia's population was seventeen million; that same year in India, around fourteen million children under the age of ten died from illness or starvation. Adopting one child would be a mere drop in the ocean, but it was something they could do. And it would make a huge difference to that one child. They chose India.

Some adoptive parents wait ten years for a child that meets their conditions. They might want a baby to raise from infancy, or specifically a boy or a girl of a particular age. Mum and Dad felt it was an important part of their stance that they offer help to whoever needed it rather than have someone picked on the basis of their preferences. So they simply said they wanted "a child."

The motto of ISSA, run by the wonderful Mrs. Saroj Sood, is: "Somewhere a child is waiting. Somewhere a family is waiting. We at ISSA bring them together." And in our case it really was as simple as that. Only a few weeks after submitting their application, Mum and Dad received a call to say they had been allocated a child named Saroo, who didn't know his surname or anything else much about his origins. Mum says that from the moment they saw a copy of the picture ISSA had taken of me for a court document, they felt I was theirs.

Mum was delighted when the word came through but also calm: somewhere inside her, she'd always felt that the vision she'd had at the age of twelve had meant it was her destiny to have an adopted child by her side. It seemed like fate had required them to wait sixteen years after deciding to adopt for me, specifically, to be ready and waiting for them. After that, things happened quickly: it was only seven months after they applied to adopt and scarcely three months after their approval that I arrived.

Mum believes that helping children who are in harsh circumstances in other countries—through sponsorship or adoption—is something more Australians should think about doing. The stress of the bureaucratic problems that delayed Mantosh's adoption affected her very badly; in fact, she became dangerously ill as a result. She is an advocate of replacing Australia's various state laws on intercountry adoption with a simplified federal law. She's critical of governments making it too difficult to adopt and feels that if it was a little easier, maybe more families would do it.

Mum's story makes me feel impossibly lucky, even blessed. She became stronger because of her tough childhood, and has taken those experiences and made something worthwhile out of them. I hope to be able to do the same, as I'm sure does Mantosh. Mum's sympathy for children who have had terrible childhoods made her a terrific mother to the children she adopted and an inspiration to us as adults. I love her for the person she is, but above all I respect her for the way she's gone about her life and the decisions she and Dad made. Certainly, I'll always be profoundly grateful to both my parents for the life they've given me.

7.

Growing Up

By the time I began high school, the map of India was still on my wall, but I hardly noticed it next to my posters of the Red Hot Chili Peppers. I was growing up Australian—a proud Tassie.

Of course, I hadn't forgotten my past or stopped thinking about my Indian family. I was still determined not to forget any details of my childhood and often went through my memories in my head, as though telling myself a story. I prayed that my mother was still alive and well. Sometimes I would lie in bed, visualizing the streets of my hometown, seeing myself walking home through them, opening the door and watching over my mother and Shekila as they slept. Transported there in my mind, I would concentrate on sending them a message that I was okay and they shouldn't worry. It was almost a meditation. But these memories were the background of my life, not the forefront. I dove into my teenage years pretty much as any other kid might.

At secondary school there were a lot more kids from other ethnic backgrounds than in primary school—particularly Greeks, Chinese, and other Indians—so any apparent differences had dissolved. I made good friends, joined a school rock band as guitarist, and still participated in lots of activities, particularly soccer, swimming, and track and field. And because the high school was quite small, it helped Mantosh settle down, too, since more attention was given to children that needed help.

I remained pretty independent, though, and did my own thing. By the age of fourteen, I was running off to the local pier with my friends to fool around and drink on the sly. I had a girlfriend, too. I wouldn't say I was particularly wild, but I was spending more and more time goofing off. It's tempting to attribute this stage of my life to my childhood and adoption, but frankly I think I just got swept away in the things that most teenagers discover.

I'd never been particularly scholarly, but my school marks began to suffer with all my extracurricular pursuits—both sporting and social. Eventually I came up against the limit of my parents' tolerance. Mum and Dad were determined, hardworking people, and it seemed to them that I was coasting along a little aimlessly. They gave me an ultimatum: leave school before Year

12 and get a job (as Mantosh later chose); work hard and get into university; or join the armed forces.

This ultimatum was a shock. The idea of the military, in particular, alarmed me, as was exactly my parents' intention. It sounded like an institutional life all too reminiscent of the homes for lost children in India that I had worked so hard to put behind me. The proposition also had a more positive effect—it reminded me of how badly I'd wanted to learn when I was in India. Here I was, being given a life filled with opportunities that I could never have imagined. I was certainly enjoying it, but maybe I wasn't making the most of it.

That was incentive enough to knuckle down: from then on I became a model student, shutting myself in my room after school to review the lessons, improving my marks, and even rising to the top of some classes. Once I finished school, I chose a three-year accounting diploma at TAFE (technical college), with a view to using that to leverage entrance to university. I also got a job in hospitality.

Mum and Dad's wake-up call was not meant to pressure me to follow any particular path, and they never made me feel that I owed them anything for adopting me. As long as I was applying myself, they would support my decisions. They would have been pleased to have seen me finish the diploma, but instead of going on to university, I found that I was enjoying the money and sociability of hospitality work so much that I was happy to leave accounting behind.

For several years, I combined work and play—I had various jobs in bars, clubs, and restaurants around Hobart, and these were good times, spinning bottles like Tom Cruise in *Cocktail* and promoting band nights. But when I saw my colleagues getting stuck in the rut of our business with no prospects, I knew I wanted more. I decided to get a degree in hospitality management, which I hoped would lead to more senior roles, and was fortunate enough to receive a scholarship to go to the Australian International Hotel School in Canberra. Because of my on-the-job experience, they knocked a three-year course back to a year and a half.

Although at the time I was still living at home, I was usually working, studying, or at the home of my girlfriend, whom I'd met in college. So when it came time to move out, the prospect wasn't a momentous one. My parents seemed pleased that I was taking the initiative. So it seemed a natural step for us all when I packed my bags and moved to Canberra, southwest of Sydney, about a three-hour flight away from Hobart. As it turned out, it was the best decision I could have made. In Canberra, my mind was unexpectedly turned again to India, and I began to think about how I might search for my childhood home.

When I moved into a residence hall at the college in Canberra in 2007, I quickly discovered that not only were there a lot of international students, but they were mostly Indian. The majority were from Delhi and what were by then known as Mumbai and Kolkata.

I'd known other Indian kids at high school, but like me, they'd grown up in Australia. Getting to know this group of people was a completely different experience. They spoke English with me, but among themselves they spoke Hindi, the first time I'd heard it in years. My native language was almost completely forgotten—the Indians at high school had only spoken English, too—and so initially I experienced a kind of reverse culture shock. In the company of the international students, for the first time I was stripped of my "Indianness"—rather than being somewhat exotic, I was the Australian among the Indians.

I was drawn to them for the basic reason that they were from the same place as I was, some of them from the very city in which I'd been lost. They had trod the same streets and had been on the same trains. They responded to my interest in them and welcomed me into their social circles. It was with this group of people that, at the age of twenty-six, I began for the first time to genuinely explore being Indian. I don't mean in a political or academic way, or in the awkward manner of the well-meaning associations my parents had tried out. I began to feel comfortable just living in my fellow Indian students' culture and company. We'd eat Indian food and go clubbing together, take trips to nearby towns, or gather at someone's house to watch Hindi masala movies—those wonderful Bollywood blends of action, romance, comedy, and drama. It wasn't false or forced; it was just a natural way of being. And the people I met weren't associated with adoption agencies or trauma. They were just regular people who happened to be from India. They encouraged me to relearn some of my native tongue, and I also found out about some of the rapid changes that had gone on in modernizing India.

In turn, I told them my own story. It was completely different describing my time in the train station to people who knew it as Kolkata's massive Howrah Station, and the river next to it as the Hooghly River. My new friends—especially those from Kolkata, who understood something of the childhood I had led—were gobsmacked. They wanted to know the details: how, what, where, when? I replied with as much information as I could.

Two things happened as a result of these conversations. First, my past became much more present—which is to say that it returned to the forefront of my mind—than it had been in years. Although I always kept my memories intact by reviewing them mentally, I hadn't spoken much about them for a long time. I'd told people here and there, mainly girlfriends, but very few—not because I was ashamed of it or wanted to keep it a secret, but because it didn't seem that important anymore. Each time I told someone, there were a lot of questions that had to be answered, and I felt it changed their view of me in much more fundamental ways than the situation deserved. I became Saroo-who-used-to-live-on-the-streets-in-Calcutta rather than just Saroo, and mostly I wanted to be the Saroo that I'd come to be. The Saroo that was lighthearted, trustworthy, a good listener, and fun to be with.

Now I was telling my story to people who knew the places I was talking about, which was different. I'm sure it changed their view of me, but I told it to increase the understanding between us rather than to open up a gap. And to talk about it like this made my past more immediate. Telling other Australian people had been a little abstract, as though talking about a fairy tale, however much they sympathized and tried to imagine what it had been like. But telling these people, who had firsthand experience of the same places, made it much more real.

Second, telling my story to people who were actually from India brought out the detectives in them. The whereabouts of my hometown was a mystery they wanted to solve, and they asked me lots of questions. Through their eyes, for the first time since I'd been in Howrah Station, I saw the possibility of working it out. Here was a bunch of people who knew the country well—the adults I'd searched for on the railway platform twenty years before. Maybe they could help me now.

So I tried out my meager collection of clues on my friends. It was the first time in many, many years that I had conjured up my ignorant five-year-old's understanding of the geography of my childhood. There was "Ginestlay," which might have been the name of my town, but which might equally have been the area or even the street. And then there was the nearby station where I'd boarded the train alone, called something like "Berampur."

I reminded my friends that the Kolkata authorities had tried and failed to work out my origins with these fragments, but they still thought it was a good start. I admitted I was hazy on exactly how long I'd been stuck on the train, but that I was certain I had boarded at night and thought I had arrived in Kolkata the next day before noon—it was certainly daytime. Although traumatic experiences such as those I'd had living on the streets seemed to be imprinted on my mind with great detail, the first big trauma—being trapped alone on a train, realizing I was powerless to stop my being dragged farther from home—appeared instead to have overwhelmed me. I recalled it more in snapshots of distress. But I had always felt that I had probably traveled for between twelve and fifteen hours, based on my memory of the light and the busyness of my surroundings when I got on and off.

One of my new friends was a girl called Amreen. When I came to know her a little better, I asked her if she could help me. I knew her dad had worked for Indian Railways in New Delhi for most of his life, and I thought perhaps he might know the train station in my hometown.

"Hey, Amreen, are you able to ask your dad if he could help me find a place called 'Berampur'? Or 'Ginestlay'?" I gave her the names of the places I remembered, probably about half a day away from Kolkata.

"Sure, I'll ask him. Anything to help," she replied.

I was excited and agitated—this was as close to help as I'd ever been.

A week later, Amreen's father responded. "I've never heard of 'Ginestlay,' but there's a suburb of Kolkata called Brahmapur. There is also a city called Baharampur in a more remote region of the same eastern state of West Bengal, and a city in the state of Orissa, down the east coast, formerly known as Berhampur and now also named Brahmapur."

"Thanks so much! This is a big help," I replied.

The first one—the suburb actually in Kolkata—was obviously not the one. But it made me wonder why no one I'd asked at Howrah Station had thought this was the place I was after. Maybe my pronunciation was wrong, or else they hadn't paused for long enough to listen to what I was saying.

The second and third places didn't seem much more likely. I didn't think they were far enough away from Howrah Station for the journey I'd been on, although I supposed it was possible I'd been on a circuitous route. The Orissan city was less than ten kilometers from the east coast, but I'd never seen the ocean until I flew over it to Australia—I'd once gone on a memorable trip to watch the sun set over a lake not far from my hometown in India, but the sight of the open sea below the plane astonished me.

Could I have grown up so close to the coast but never known it? On the other hand, my friends thought that, based on the way I looked, I might have come from West Bengal, which was tucked in the eastern part of the country next to Bangladesh. That reminded me that when I was growing up in Hobart, Mum had told me some elderly Indians we met had thought it likely I came from the east. *Could I be remembering the train journey wrong? Might the time and distance have been exaggerated in the mind of a frightened five-year-old?*

Little seeds of doubt were being sown in my mind.

In addition to the hunches of my friends, I started to use the Internet to search for more information. We'd had Internet at home since my later years at school, but it was a very different medium from what it is today. It was much slower, of course, especially in the pre-broadband dial-up days, but what we call the Internet now was only just getting started as "the Web" when I was finishing school. Tools like Wikipedia were in their infancy by the time I started college. Today it's hard to imagine that you could fail to turn up information on any topic at all—regardless of how obscure—but it wasn't long ago that the Internet was more the preserve of geeks and academics.

This was also before social media, when it was not common to connect with people you didn't already know. E-mail was a more formal communication tool, not something with which you could reach out to the world anonymously. Adding to the fact that I wasn't thinking much about my Indian past, it just hadn't crossed my mind before that this reasonably new invention could be of some use to me.

At college I had twenty-four-hour access to the Internet and my own computer in my room. So I started searching for any kind of information I could find using various spellings of "Ginestlay," with no success or at least not the kind of success that I could make any real sense of. The "Berampur"-type names were similarly inconclusive—too many possibilities and nothing much to go on.

If I'd begun to have doubts about my memories of these names and the length of time I was on the train, I had none about my memories of my family, or the town and the streets I'd walked as a child. I could close my eyes and see clearly the train station in "Berampur," where I climbed aboard the train: the position of the platform, the big pedestrian overpass at one end, and the large water tower on its high platform rising above. I knew that if I could just see any of the places that had been suggested by my friends or my search engine, or if I could somehow see what someone thought was my hometown, I could tell straightaway if it was. It was the names that I couldn't be sure of.

Maps didn't help, either. I knew that somewhere among all the names and lines was my home, if only I knew the right place to look, but the only maps I could find weren't big enough to show small villages, let alone neighborhoods or the detailed street plans I needed. All I could do was look for names that seemed similar, scanning likely areas based on their proximity to Kolkata and my own appearance. And even if I found a town name similar to "Berampur" or "Ginestlay," how could I tell if our tumbledown dwelling or the right train station was there? For a while, I even toyed with the idea of flying to West Bengal to search on the ground, but that wasn't a very serious proposition. How long could I possibly ramble through parts of India looking for a familiar clue? The place was enormous. It was too much like jumping on random trains at Howrah Station.

Then I became aware of a map that actually *would* allow me to roam across the landscape, and what was even better was that I could do it from the security of my study chair: Google Earth.

Many people probably remember their first experience of Google Earth. Its satellite imaging meant anyone could look at the world from above, sweeping across it like an astronaut. You could view whole continents, countries, or cities, or search for place-names and then zoom down on the spots you were interested in, rendered in astonishing detail—up close to the Eiffel Tower, or Ground Zero, or your own house. In fact, that seemed to be what everyone typically did first—zeroed in on where they lived and saw what it looked like from above, like a bird or a god. When I heard what Google Earth could do, my heart raced.

Might my childhood home be visible if I worked out where to look? Google Earth was the perfect tool. It was almost as if it had been invented just for me. I got on my computer and began searching.

As I'd never got even a flicker of recognition from anyone about "Ginestlay," I thought that the place sounding like "Berampur" was the most solid reference I had. And if I found it, my hometown would be close by along the train line. So I searched for places like "Berampur" and, as always, the results were numerous—there were a large number of variations of the name strung across the length and breadth of India, and multiple places sharing some of them. Brahmapur, Baharampur, Berhampur, Berhampore, Birampur, Burhampoor, Brahmpur . . . on and on they went.

It seemed sensible to start with the two places Amreen's father had suggested, in West Bengal and Orissa. Slowly but surely, aerial images of each town appeared on the screen—the way Google Earth worked was exactly as I'd hoped. With this tool, I would be able to see any landmarks I remembered, and hopefully identify the right place almost as easily as if I were there in person, or at least as if I were there in a hot air balloon. Looking down at a place from above meant twisting your mind a little to imagine it from the street.

Baharampur in West Bengal had a couple of train stations, but they didn't have the overpass I distinctly remembered, and there didn't appear to be any place on the lines out of town with a name like "Ginestlay," either. One line also ran close to several large lakes that I was sure would be visible from a train, but I'd never seen anything like them where I'd been. In fact, the surroundings of the town didn't seem right at all—the place I was looking for had a range of hills nearby that the train line ran through, which I couldn't see close to this place, and everything looked too green and lush. The region I came from was a patchwork of farmland around dusty towns. I had to concede that changes could have occurred since my time there—maybe more irrigation had been brought in and the region had become greener. But the other factors seemed to rule it out.

The city in Orissa, Brahmapur, seemed to be in a drier region, but its station had very long covered platforms on either side of the tracks, which was different from the simpler configuration I remembered. There was no water tower to be seen, either; instead, there were lots of silos of some kind, which I had no memory of. Once again there was no "Ginestlay" along the lines near this place. And seeing an image of how close the sea was to the city made me certain I couldn't have been unaware of it.

That neither of these looked right was no reason to give up hope since there were still so many other places to look at, but it was disheartening. And it made me consider how much things might have changed since I'd been there. Stations might have been refurbished or rebuilt, roads changed nearby, towns grown.

Courtesy of ISSA, Kolkata

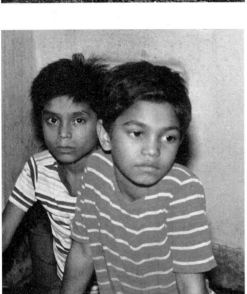

After being picked up off the streets of Kolkata in 1987, I spent two months at the Nava Jeevan orphanage, run by the Indian Society for Sponsorship and Adoption (ISSA). I'm in the striped T-shirt *(left)*, with my friend Asra standing beside me on the caged front porch *(right)*. ISSA ran lost notices in the newspapers *(top)*, unaware that my home was much farther away from the areas they were trying to reach.

The photo book prepared by my new parents, the Brierleys, which I was shown at Nava Jeevan to familiarize myself with them and my new home.

THIS IS THE CITY
WHERE WE LIVE —

FOR SAROO,
NAVA JEEVAN
PGT, RANGANATHPUR COLONY
THAKURPUKUR, CALCUTTA

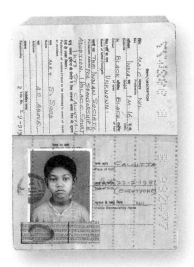

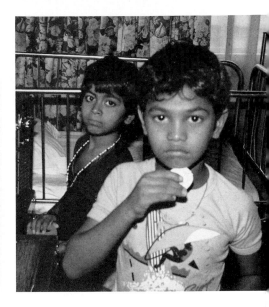

With a passport featuring an invented birthday of May 22, 1981, I left for Australia with other adoptees and official escorts, including ISSA's Saroj Sood, sitting with Asra and me on her lap. This was my first experience of the eye-opening luxury of hotels.

I arrived in Melbourne's Tullamarine Airport in my Tasmania T-shirt and proceeded with the escorts and other children to a VIP room, where our new parents were waiting. Mum and Dad welcomed me with a book and a stuffed koala bear. I'm still holding the remains of the chocolate bar we were given on the plane—my first word to my new parents was "Cadbury."

The first maps in my life—the wall map of India I grew up with in my room (seen here as it was prepared for my arrival), and the map of my hometown that my mother drew with me in her notebook when at age seven I first told her the story of how I became lost.

I had a happy life growing up in Hobart with my new family, which soon included my younger adopted brother, Mantosh. Below, he sits at the computer next to my friend and fellow Nava Jeevan adoptee, Asra, who occasionally visited from Victoria. Like many teenagers, I had rock star ambitions.

I didn't know the name of my childhood hometown. But several years at the computer, searching with Google Earth, led to my incredible discoveries: first, Burhanpur Railway Station *(above)*—with its familiar water tower—from which I accidentally boarded the train that took me across the country; and then, up to the line, the familiar layout of my hometown itself *(below)*.

From the satellite view of my search to returning to India to retrace my steps on the ground: the dam by the rail bridge on the southern outskirts of my hometown *(opposite, top left)*; the park fountain, the rail underpass, and the railway station *(opposite)*; and the now-abandoned home in which I grew up in the town's poor neighborhood *(above)*. Today I dwarf the front door.

My mother, Kamla, and I were reunited after twenty-six years at her modest dwelling *(right)* just around the corner from where we used to live. She had remained in the neighborhood in the hope I might one day return.

Reuniting with my family was an overwhelming experience. My older brother, Kallu, and younger sister, Shekila, returned home to meet me.

The train carriage I was trapped on was something like the one above and at right—although in those days, the benches on second-class carriages were wooden and not cushioned. I will never be exactly certain of the route I was taken on across India from Burhanpur to Kolkata, but I made the journey again as an adult with a top-class ticket *(top)*.

In Kolkata, I found Saroj Sood *(above, seated far left)* in the same ISSA office from which she'd arranged my adoption a quarter of a century before. My ISSA file notes: "We consulted Saru if he would like us to look for a new family for him, and to this he agreed readily." In the next room *(below left)*, new orphans napped on floor mats.

It was all too easy to see how a small child was ignored inside the huge and busy Howrah Station *(above)*. Below are the imposing walls and iron gates of the Liluah juvenile home, where I was originally sent after being picked up off the streets. It is now a home for women and girls only, so I wasn't permitted to take photographs inside.

In my first weeks on the streets, I never strayed far from the distinctive red block of Howrah Station, seen from Howrah Bridge *(below)*. The bridge is a monumental structure, which loomed over me when I survived weeks living on or around the banks of the Hooghly River.

My two families, which make me feel doubly blessed. *(Top)* Mum and Dad (John and Sue Brierley) and my brother, Mantosh. *(Bottom)* Rear, from left: my brother, Kallu, his wife, Nasim, their daughter, Norin, my mother, Kamla, and my sister, Shekila. Front, from left: Shekila's son, Ayan, and Kallu's sons Shail and Sameer.

If too much had changed, I might not find it easy to recognize the station I was looking for after all.

Despite the comprehensive nature of this new resource—or because of it—it was clear that searching for my home was going to be a mammoth task. If I wasn't certain about the place-names, I couldn't rely on the search function to deliver the answer. And even if I stumbled upon the right area, perhaps I wouldn't be able to recognize it from the air. How could I be certain about anything? On top of all that, Internet speeds and computers were much slower then—Google Earth was an incredible tool but a massive one, and using it to look over great distances would be hugely time-consuming.

If I was going to take my studies seriously, I wouldn't be able to spend all my time scouring Google Earth. So after the initial excitement, I told myself I was just mucking about and tried not to get too distracted by it. I put some time into checking out a few places, concentrating on the northeast regions around Kolkata on and off for several months. But I didn't find anything familiar.

For a while, some of my friends got used to my announcing that I'd given up the search, only to admit later that it was still playing on my mind. Many of the original Indian sleuths had returned home, and others let the issue go when it seemed I might not be as troubled by it as they had first thought.

Eventually, I let the whole thing slide. The quest started to seem a little abstract. It was hard to feel I was making any progress—I was searching for the needle in the haystack, and the task seemed beyond the commitment I could give it. I was at college to study, which required a great deal of my attention, and I didn't want to squander it as a hermit at a computer the rest of the time. Some well-meaning people even warned me that the search could drive me crazy. I'd grown up an Australian man in a loving family. Fate had delivered me from dire straits into a comfortable existence—perhaps I needed to accept that the past was past and move on.

I realize now that I was also a little scared and defensive of my memories—I'd lived with them for so long, and clung to them so tightly, that I wanted very passionately to preserve them and the kernel of hope they contained. If I went back and searched, and failed to find anything, would that mean I really did have to draw a line through the past and move on? If I could find no trace of my home and family, how would I keep holding on to their memory? Going back without certainty might ruin the little I had.

With the trail cool, I completed my course and moved back to Hobart in 2009, and found a bar job to support myself. Despite the diploma in my back pocket, it only took a few weeks for me to realize I'd lost interest in the hospitality industry. I'd had an inkling this was the case while still in Canberra, but I had wanted to at least complete the qualification, having come as far as I had.

We all reach a point as young adults when we wonder what we should be doing with our lives—or, at the very least, which direction to point ourselves in. Beyond the means to get by, we need to think about what's most important to us. Not surprisingly, I discovered that for me the answer was family. Perhaps being away from Hobart for a while had strengthened this feeling. And my renewed interest in my past had prompted me to think about my relationship with my family in Hobart. It occurred to me that the Brierley family business might give me an opportunity to draw aspects of my life together, and I was excited when my parents agreed.

Mum and Dad own a business selling industrial hoses and fittings, valves, and pumps. In a remarkable coincidence, Dad started the business the day I arrived from India—he left my granddad in the brand-new office to answer any calls when he set off to Melbourne with Mum to meet me.

Joining the business meant working with Dad every day, and I quickly realized that I'd made the right choice. Working with him was inspirational. I think that some of his determination, work ethic, and focus on success rubbed off on me. He certainly kept me busy, and the experience brought us even closer. Mantosh later took the same path, so now the Brierley men all work together.

At the same time, I threw myself into a new relationship with a woman that I'd met through friends. Eventually, my girlfriend and I moved in together. The move back to Hobart and all that followed reminded me that tracing my roots was not the most important thing in my life, overriding all else. I understand that this may sound strange to some people. Adoptees, whether or not they ever knew their birth parents, often describe the constant, gnawing feeling of there being something missing: without a connection, or at least the knowledge of where they are from, they feel incomplete. But I didn't feel that. I never forgot my Indian mother and family—and I never will—but being separated from them didn't create a block that somehow prevented me from pursuing a full and happy life. I'd learned quickly, as a matter of survival, that I needed to take opportunities as they came—if they came—and to look forward to the future. Part of that was gratefully accepting the life I was granted through my adoption. So I tried to concentrate again on that which I have been so blessed to have been given.

8.

———

Resuming the Search

By now, I should have been used to life's many unexpected twists and turns. But things still manage to take me completely by surprise, and though I might have become better than some at coping with new circumstances—changes of career, of location, even of fortune—emotional changes can hit me as hard as they do anyone else. Perhaps even a little harder.

Working with Dad and learning to be a salesman was great—I do it to this day—but my relationship with my girlfriend proved tempestuous and we went through a difficult breakup. Although I was the one to end it, I found myself bereft and full of regret. I moved back into my parents' home and went through a dark period of conflicting emotions: rejection, disappointment, bitterness, loneliness, and a sense of failure. I sometimes didn't make it to work or made careless errors. My parents wondered when I'd pull myself back together to be the positive, forward-looking man into which they thought I'd developed.

I was lucky to have made good friends over the years. A fortuitous meeting with Byron, a guy I'd known from my hospitality days, ended with him suggesting I move into a spare room at his place for a while. He had become a doctor and he introduced me to a new crowd. His kindness and the fresh faces I met really helped pick me up. If family has been the most important thing in my life, friends have not been far behind.

Byron was always going out and enjoying himself, and I liked to join him occasionally, but I was also glad to spend some time alone at home. Although I'd become much less depressed since right after the breakup, I was still thinking about it and wondering how to think of myself as an individual rather than as part of a couple. And although I don't think my childhood made this process any easier or harder, it got me thinking once again in earnest about my life in India.

Byron had broadband Internet access at home and I had a new, fast laptop. Even in the periods when I hadn't felt that retracing my past was imperative, I'd never forgotten about it or ruled it out completely. In this new phase of my life, I had a fuller connection with my parents through the family business, and even felt I was giving back to them a little. That gave me the security to face the emotional risks of the search again. Yes, there was a lot to lose—each failure to find my childhood home chipped away at the certainty of my memories—but there was also much to gain. I wondered whether I might be avoiding the search, and also if the confidence I'd had that my past wasn't affecting my ability to get on with the rest of my life was perhaps overstated. At the very least, was this just my failure to buckle down, much like my teenage drifting? And what if, by the slimmest of chances, I managed to find my old home? How could I pass up the chance of discovering where I was from, and maybe even finding my birth mother?

I decided that resuming the search—in a low-key way—would be part of regaining a positive outlook on life. Maybe the past could help shape the future.

Alas, the new search didn't start out as an obsession.

If Byron wasn't home, I might spend a couple of hours musing over the various "B" towns again. Or I might make a casual sweep down the east coast, to see what was there. I even checked out a Birampur in Uttar Pradesh, near Delhi, in the central north of India, but that was a ridiculously long way from Kolkata, and I couldn't have traveled that far in twelve or so hours. It turned out it doesn't even have a train station.

These occasional forays showed the folly of searching by town, particularly when I wasn't sure about the names. If I was going to do this, I needed to be strategic and methodical about it.

I went over what I knew. I came from a place where Muslims and Hindus lived in close proximity and where Hindi was spoken. Those things were true of most of India. I recalled all those warm nights outside, under the stars, which at least suggested it wouldn't be in the colder regions of the far north. I hadn't lived by the sea, although I couldn't rule out that I'd lived near it. And I hadn't lived in the mountains. My hometown had a railway station—India was riddled with train lines, but they didn't run through every single village and town.

Then there was the opinion of the Indians at college that I looked like someone from the east, perhaps around West Bengal. I had my doubts: in the eastern part of the country, the region took in some of the Himalayas, which wasn't right, and part of the Ganges Delta, which looked much too lush and fertile to be my home. But as these were people who had firsthand experience of India, it seemed silly to dismiss their hunch.

I also thought I could remember enough landmark features to recognize my hometown if I came across it, or to at least narrow the field. I clearly recalled the bridge over the river where we played as kids and the nearby dam wall that restricted the river's flow below it. I knew how to get from the train station to our house, and I knew the layout of the station.

The other station I thought I remembered quite well was the

"B" one, where I'd boarded the train. Although I'd been there quite a few times with my brothers, they'd never let me leave it, so I knew nothing of the town outside the station—all I'd ever seen beyond the exit was a sort of small ring road for horse carts and cars, and a road beyond it that led into the town. But still, there were a couple of distinguishing features. I remembered the station building and that it had only a couple of tracks, on the other side of which was a big water tank on a tower. There was also a pedestrian overpass across the tracks. And just before the train pulled into town from the direction of my home, it crossed a small gorge.

So I had some vague thoughts on likely regions, and some ways of identifying "Ginestlay" and the "B" place if I found them. Now I needed a better search method. I realized that the names of places had been a distraction, or were at least not the right place to start. Instead, I thought about the end of the journey. I knew that train lines linked the "B" place with Kolkata. Logic dictated, then, that if I followed all the train lines out of Kolkata, I would eventually find my starting point. And from there, my hometown was itself up the line, not far away. I might even come upon my home first, depending on how the lines linked up. This was an intimidating prospect—there were many, many train lines from the national hub of Kolkata's Howrah Station, and my train might have zigzagged across any of the lines of the spider's web. It was unlikely to be a simple, straight route.

Still, even with the possibility of some winding, irregular paths out of Howrah, there was also a limit to how far I could have been transported in the time frame. I'd spent, I thought, a long time on the train—somewhere between twelve and fifteen hours. If I made some calculations, I could narrow the search field, ruling out places too far away.

Why hadn't I thought of the search with this clarity before? Maybe I had been too overwhelmed by the scale of the problem to think straight, too consumed by what I didn't know to focus on what I did. But as it dawned on me that I could turn this into a painstaking, deliberate task that simply required dedication, something clicked inside. If all it took were time and patience to find home, with the aid of Google Earth's god's-eye view, then I would do it. Seeing it almost as much an intellectual challenge as an emotional quest, I threw myself into solving it.

First, I worked on the search zone. How fast could India's diesel trains travel, and would that have changed much since the eighties? I thought my Indian friends from college might be able to help, especially Amreen, whose father would likely have a more educated guess, so I got in touch with them. The general consensus was around seventy or eighty kilometers an hour. That seemed like a good start. Figuring I had been trapped on the train for around twelve to fifteen hours, overnight, I calculated how many kilometers I might have traveled in that time, which I put at around a thousand, or approximately 620 miles.

So the place I was looking for was a thousand kilometers along a train line out of Howrah Station. On Google Earth you can draw lines on the map at precise distances, so I made a circular boundary line of a thousand kilometers around Kolkata and saved it for my searches. That meant that as well as West Bengal, my search field included the states of Jharkhand, Chhattisgarh, and nearly half of the central state of Madhya Pradesh to the west; Orissa to the south; Bihar and a third of Uttar Pradesh to the north; and most of the northeastern spur of India, which encircles Bangladesh. (I knew I wasn't from Bangladesh, as I'd have spoken Bengali, not Hindi. This was confirmed when I discovered that a rail connection between the two countries had only been established a few years ago.)

It was a staggering amount of territory, covering some 962,300 square kilometers, over a quarter of India's huge landmass. Within its bounds lived 345 million people. I tried to keep my emotions out of the exercise, but I couldn't help but wonder: Is it possible to find my four family members among these 345 million? Even though my calculations were reliant on guesswork and were therefore very rough, and even though that still presented me with a huge field within which to search, it felt like I was narrowing things down. Rather than randomly throwing the haystack around to find the needle, I could concentrate on picking through a manageable portion and set it aside if it proved empty.

The train lines within the search zone wouldn't all simply stretch out to the edge in a straight radius, of course—there would be a lot of twists, turns, and junctions, as they wound around and traveled much more than a thousand kilometers before they reached the boundary edge. So I planned to work outward from Kolkata, the only point of the journey I was certain about.

The first time I zoomed in on Howrah Station, looking at the rows of ridged gray platform roofs and all the tracks spilling out of it like the fraying end of a rope, I was amazed and shocked that I'd once trod barefoot along these walkways. I had to open my eyes wide to make sure what I was looking at was real. I was about to embark on a high-tech version of what I'd done in my first week there, twenty years ago, randomly taking trains out to see if they went back home.

I took a deep breath, chose a train line, and started scrolling along it.

Immediately, it became clear that progress would be slow. Even with broadband, my laptop had to render the image, which took time. It started a little pixelated, then resolved into an aerial photograph. I was looking for landmarks I recognized and paid particular attention to the stations, as they were the places I remembered most vividly.

When I first zoomed out to see how far I'd gone along the track, I was amazed at how little progress the hours of scrolling and studying had brought me. But rather than being frustrated and impatient, I found I had enormous confidence that I would find what I was looking for as long as I was thorough. That gave me a great sense of calm as I resumed my search. In fact, it quickly became compelling, and I returned to it several nights a week. Before I turned in each night, I'd mark how far I'd gone on a track and save the search, then resume from that point at the next opportunity.

I would come across goods yards, overpasses and under-passes, bridges over rivers, and junctions. Sometimes I skipped along a bit but then nervously went back to repeat a section, reminding myself that if I wasn't methodical, I could never be sure I'd looked everywhere. I didn't jump ahead to look for sta-tions in case I missed a small one—I followed the tracks so I could check out anything that came along. And if I found myself reaching the edge of the boundary I'd devised, I'd go back along the train line to a previous junction and then head off in another direction.

I remember one night early on, following a line north, I came to a river crossing not far outside a town. I caught my breath as I zoomed in closer. The dam wall was decaying, but maybe the area had since been reconstructed? I quickly dragged the cursor to roll the image along. Did the countryside look right? It was quite green, but there were a lot of farms on the outskirts of my town. I watched as the town unpixelated before my eyes. It was quite small. Too small, surely. But with a child's perspective . . . And there was a high pedestrian overpass across the tracks near the station! But what were the large blank areas dotted around the town? Three lakes, four or five even, within the tiny village's bounds—and it was suddenly obvious that this wasn't the place. You didn't clear whole neighborhoods to put in lakes. And of course, many, many stations were likely to have overpasses, and many towns would be situated near life-giving rivers, which the tracks would have to cross. How many times would I wonder if all the landmarks aligned, only to be left with tired, sore eyes and the realization that I was mistaken again?

Weeks and then months passed with my spending hours at a time every couple of nights on the laptop. Byron made sure I spent other nights out in the real world so I didn't become an Internet recluse. I covered the countryside of West Bengal and Jharkhand in these early stages without finding anything familiar, but at least it meant that much of the immediate vicinity of Kolkata could be ruled out. Despite the hunch of my Indian friends, I'd come from farther away.

Several months later, I was lucky enough to meet someone with whom I started a new relationship, which made the search less of a priority for a while. Lisa and I met in 2010 through a friend of Byron's and mine. We became friends on Facebook, and then I asked her for her phone number. We hit it off immediately; Lisa's background is in business management and she is smart, pretty, and can hold a great conversation. However, we had an unsettled start together, with a couple of breakups and reunions, which meant there was a similar inconsistency in the periods I spent looking on the Internet, before we finally settled into the lasting relationship we have today.

I didn't know how a girlfriend would take to the time-consuming quest of her partner staring at maps on a laptop. But Lisa understood the personal and growing importance of the search, and was patient and supportive. She was as amazed as anyone about my past, and wanted me to find the answers I was looking for. We moved into a small flat together in 2010. I thought of the nights I spent there on the laptop as being a pastime, like playing computer games. But Lisa says that even then, with our relationship in full swing, I was obsessive. Looking back, I can see that this was true.

After all the years of my story being in my thoughts and dreams, I felt I was closing in on the reality. I decided this time I wasn't going to listen to anybody who said, "It might be time to move on," or "It's just not possible to find your hometown in all of India like this." Lisa never said those things, and with her support, I became even more determined to succeed.

I didn't tell many people what I was doing anyway. And I decided not to tell my parents. I was worried they might misunderstand my intentions. I didn't want them to think that the intensity of my search revealed an unhappiness with the life they'd given me or the way they'd raised me. I also didn't want them to think that I was wasting time. So even as it took up more and more of my life, I kept it mostly to myself. I finished work with Dad at five p.m., and by five thirty I would be back at the laptop, slowly advancing along train tracks and studying the towns they led to. This went on for months—it had been over a year since I started. But I reasoned that even if it took years . . . or decades . . . it was possible to eventually sift completely through a haystack. The needle would have to show up if I persisted.

Slowly, over several more months, I eliminated whole areas of India. I traced all the connections within the northeastern states without finding anything familiar, and I was confident that I could rule out Orissa, too. Determined to be thorough, no matter how long it took, I started following lines farther out than my original thousand-kilometer zone. South beyond Orissa, I eliminated Andhra Pradesh, five hundred kilometers farther down the east coast. Jharkhand and Bihar didn't offer up anything promising, either, and as I wound up in Uttar Pradesh, I thought I'd keep going to cover most of the state. In fact, the states eventually replaced my zone boundary as a way of marking my progress. Ruling out areas state by state provided a series of goals that spurred me on.

Unless I had something pressing to do for work, or some other unbreakable commitment, I was on the laptop seven nights a week. I went out with Lisa sometimes, of course, but the moment we got home I was back on the computer. Sometimes I caught her looking at me strangely, as though she thought I might have gone a bit crazy. She'd say, "You're at it again!" but I would reply, "I have to . . . I'm really sorry!" I think Lisa knew she simply had to let me exhaust myself of the interest. I became distant during that time, and although Lisa would have been within her rights to feel alone in this still-new relationship, we worked through it. Perhaps, to some extent, sharing something so fundamental to me strengthened our connection—and that came through when we sometimes talked about what it all meant. It wasn't always easy for me to articulate, especially as I was trying to keep a lid on my expectations, trying to convince myself it was a fascinating exercise, not a deeply meaningful personal quest. Talking to Lisa sometimes revealed the underlying importance of the search to me: that I was looking for my home to provide closure and to understand my past and perhaps myself better as a result, in the hope that I might somehow reconnect with my Indian family so they would know what had happened to me. Lisa understood all this and didn't resent it, even if there were times when she wanted to ban me from staring at the screen for my own sake. Once in a while she would simply come over and shut my laptop and place it on the floor because I was becoming so obsessive about my search.

At times Lisa admitted her own greatest fear: that I would find what I thought I was looking for, go back to India, and somehow be wrong or fail to find my family there. Would I return to Hobart and simply start again, obsessively searching online? I couldn't answer her questions any more than I could allay her fears. I couldn't allow myself to think about failure.

If anything, I became more intense about my search as 2010 drew to a close, and the speed of our newly acquired broadband connection made it quicker to refresh the images and zoom in and out. But I still had to take it slowly—if I rushed, I'd leave myself open to wondering later if I'd missed anything and then going back in an endless cycle. And I had to try not to bend my memories to fit what I was looking at.

By early 2011, I was concentrating more on areas within India's center, in Chhattisgarh and Madhya Pradesh. I spent months poring over them, relentlessly, methodically.

Of course, there were times when I doubted the wisdom, and even the sanity, of what I was doing. Night after night, with the day's last reserves of energy and willpower, I sat staring at rail-

way lines, searching for places my five-year-old mind might recognize. It was a repetitive, forensic exercise, and sometimes it
started to feel claustrophobic, as if I were trapped and looking
out at the world through a small window, unable to break free of
my course in a mind-twisting echo of my childhood ordeal.

And then one night in March around one in the morning, in
just such a mood, spent with frustration, I took a wild dive into
the haystack, and it changed everything.

9.

_____

Finding Home

As always, on March 31, 2011, I had come home from work, grabbed my laptop, opened Google Earth, and settled in for a session on the sofa, stopping only briefly for dinner when Lisa got home. I was examining the central west at this time, so I picked up there, "traveling" a train line near my former search-zone boundary. Even with quicker broadband, it was still slow going. I continued for what seemed like ages, looking at a few stations, but as usual, when I zoomed out, I found I'd only covered a tiny area. I thought that the countryside looked a bit green for my dusty old town, but I knew by now that India's landscape changed appearance regularly as you moved across it.

After a few hours, I had followed a line to a junction. I took a break, checking Facebook for a while before rubbing my eyes, stretching my back, and returning to my task.

Before zooming in, I idly flicked the map along to get a quick picture of where the westerly line out of the junction headed, and watched hills, forests, and rivers sweep by, a seemingly endless terrain of reasonably similar features. I was distracted by a large river that fed into what looked like a massive, deep blue lake called Nal Damayanti Sagar, which was surrounded by some lush country and had mountains to its north. For a while, I enjoyed this little exploration, indulgently unrelated to my search, like a recreational hike of grand proportions. It was getting late, after all, and I'd turn in soon.

There didn't seem to be any train lines in this part of the country, which might have been why it was relaxing to look at. But once I'd noticed that, I found myself almost subconsciously looking for one. There were villages and towns dotted around here and there, and I wondered how the people traveled without rail—perhaps they didn't move around much? And farther west, still no tracks! Then as the countryside flattened out into farmland, I finally came across a little blue symbol denoting a train station. I was so attuned to looking for them, I was somehow relieved to find this one, and I checked out the tiny wayside station: just a few buildings to the side of a reasonably major train line with several tracks. Out of habit, I started tracing the route as it wound southwest. I quickly came across another station, a bit bigger, again with a platform on only one side of the tracks, but with some areas of the township on either side. That explained the overpass, and was that . . . was that a water tower just nearby?

Holding my breath, I zoomed in for a closer look. Sure enough, it was a municipal water tank just across from the platform, and not far from a large pedestrian overpass spanning the railway line. I scrolled over to the town side and saw something incredible—a horseshoe-shaped road around a square immediately outside the station. Could it be—perhaps it was the ring road I used to be able to see from the platform! Was it possible? I closed my eyes and went back twenty-four years in time to when I would walk to the station's exit and see the ring road with an island in the middle. I thought to myself, *This is unique; I haven't seen this before.* I zoomed out, discovering that the train line skimmed the northwestern edge of a really large town. I clicked on the blue train station symbol to reveal its name . . . Burhanpur. My heart nearly stopped. *Burhanpur!*

I didn't recognize the town itself, but then I'd never been in it—I'd never left the platform. I zoomed back in and re-examined the ring road, the water tower, the overpass, and they were all positioned where I remembered them. That meant that not far away, just up the line, I should find my hometown, "Ginestlay."

Almost afraid to do so, I dragged the cursor to pull the image north along the train line. When I saw that the track crossed a gorge just on the edge of the built-up area, I was flooded with adrenaline—I remembered in a flash that the train I took with my brothers traveled on a small bridge over a gorge like that before pulling into the station. I pushed on more urgently, east then northeast, in just moments zooming over seventy kilometers of green farms, forested hills, and small rivers. Then I passed across some dry, flat land broken up by a patchwork of irrigated farmland and the occasional small village, before I hit a bridge over a substantial river. Ahead I was able to see the town's outskirts. The river's flow was significantly reduced below the bridge by dam walls on either side. If this was the right place, this was the river I used to play in, and there should be a bigger concrete dam wall to my right a little farther from the bridge. . . .

There it was!

I sat staring at the screen for what seemed like an eternity. What I was looking at matched the picture in my head exactly. I couldn't think straight; I was frozen with excitement, terrified to go on.

Finally, after a couple of minutes, I forced myself to take the next step, slowly, nervously. I tried to calm myself so I didn't jump to any rash conclusions. If I really was looking at "Ginestlay" for the first time in twenty-four years, then I should be able to follow the path I remembered from the river back to the train station, only a short way up ahead. I began to drag the cursor again, slowly rolling the map to trace the course of the path, which wound gently alongside a tributary stream, left and right, around a field, under a street overpass, and then . . . the station. I clicked on the blue symbol and the name came up on the screen: Khandwa Railway Station.

The name meant nothing to me.

My stomach knotted. How could this be?

Things had looked so right all the way from Burhanpur, which had to be the "B" town I had tried to remember. But if the bridge and the river were correct, where was "Ginestlay"? I tried not to despair. I had spent a lot of time in and around our local train station as a boy, so I checked off what I remembered—the three platforms, the covered pedestrian overpass that connected them, an underpass road beneath the tracks at the northern end. But it wasn't so much the existence of these reasonably common features but their position in relation to each other that would identify the specific place that I was looking for. It all checked out. I also remembered a huge fountain in a park near the underpass, and I went looking. Sure enough, though it was a little indistinct, I thought I detected its familiar circular shape in a central clearing surrounded by trees.

From here, I knew the route to where my home should be. This was why I'd gone over and over it in my head since I was a little boy: so that I would never forget it.

Now, as a man, I followed the road up from the fountain and along the route of the underpass, and then the streets and alleys I had walked as a child—the way I used to imagine myself walking when I lay in bed at night, in the safe comfort of my house in

Hobart, trying to project myself back to my village home to let my mother know I was okay. Before I realized I'd gone far enough, I was looking down at the neighborhood I knew as a boy.

Still, nothing like "Ginestlay" came up on the map. It was the strangest feeling, and one that I became familiar with over the next year or so—part of me was certain, but still another part of me doubted. I was sure this was the right place, but for all this time I'd also been sure of the name "Ginestlay." Khandwa rang no bells whatsoever. Maybe "Ginestlay" was a part of Khandwa? A suburb? That seemed possible. I looked through the maze of alleys where my family lived, and although the image wasn't as clear as what I would get when I looked at where I lived in Hobart, I was sure I could see the little rectangular roof of my childhood home. Of course, I'd never seen the place from above, but the building was the right shape and in precisely the correct location. I hovered over the streets for a while, astonished, trying to take it all in. Finally I couldn't contain my excitement any longer.

I called out to Lisa, "I've found my hometown! You've gotta come and see this!" It was only then that I realized the time. I'd been at the computer for over seven hours nonstop, except for dinner.

Lisa poked her head around the corner, yawning, in her nightie. It took her a moment to wake up properly, but even half-asleep she could see my excitement. "Are you sure?" she asked.

"This is it, this is it!" I replied.

In that moment, I was convinced. "This is my hometown!"

It had taken eight months of intense searching, and it was nearly five years since I'd first downloaded Google Earth.

Lisa grinned and hugged me tightly. "That's so great! You did it, Saroo!"

After a sleepless night, I went to work and saw Dad in his office. For him, the news was going to come out of the blue, and might even be a shock. I tried to rehearse what I was going to say in my head, hoping to lend it some gravity so he would realize that I really was convinced that I had found my hometown. But in the end, all I managed was to put on a stern face as I said, "Dad, I think I've found my hometown."

He stopped working on his computer. "Really? On a *map?*" I could tell he was skeptical. "You're sure?"

It was a natural response to the sheer improbability of the discovery.

What had happened? Had I suddenly remembered where I came from after all these years? I told him that I was indeed sure and how I'd found it. Dad remained doubtful, partly to protect me from the possibility that I was wrong. Caution was understandable, but I needed him to know that I was convinced and wanted him to be, too.

In retrospect, one of the reasons I was so keen for Dad to believe me was that telling him was the start of my journey back to India. Lisa was, of course, always in on my search and my hopes for it, but telling Dad made the discovery, and the need to do something about it, a reality. I didn't have firm plans about what to do next, but sharing the news made me realize that this was the start, not the end, of a journey. From that moment, it was clear that this was a life-changing discovery for all of us, even if I found out nothing more.

Telling Mum was another step. She knew I had some interest in finding my Indian home and that I looked for clues on the Internet, but not that I'd resumed an active search. I was particularly nervous and anxious about upsetting her, which is probably why I told Dad first. Mum had such a dedicated belief in adoption and the authentic family that adoption created. I was worried about how my news would affect her, and I wanted to reassure her that of course they would always be my parents.

So that same night we gathered at the family home, each of us slightly on edge. For my part, I was eager to show them the Google Earth images that had convinced me I'd found my hometown. They responded tentatively. The idea that I'd used a bird's-eye view to search one of the most populated countries on earth, looking for landmarks I remembered from when I was five, and that I'd actually found what I was looking for was unbelievable, or at the very least a tremendous surprise. I pointed out the walled dam on the southern edge of Khandwa, the train lines, and the underpass I'd walked through to get to the station, just as I had described to Mum when I was little.

I think we all wondered, at the backs of our minds, what this discovery would mean for the future. I wondered whether my parents had always thought this day would come, and feared their son would be reclaimed by India and perhaps lost to them forever, much as I was lost to my birth mother all those years ago.

They congratulated me, and we had a slightly muted celebratory dinner with lots of questions in our minds.

When I arrived home afterward, I was full of nervous energy and went straight back to my computer. Maybe I had been carried away—maybe there were other ways of confirming what I already knew. I turned to another tool that hadn't been around when I started my search—Facebook. I typed in the word "Khandwa." A group called "Khandwa: My Home Town" popped up. I sent a message to the group administrator:

Can anyone help me, i think I'm from Khandwa. i haven't seen or been back to the place for twenty-four years. Just wondering if there is a big fountain near the cinema?

The fountain was the most distinct landmark I could think of. The park where it was located was a busy meeting place, and the circular fountain had a statue on a plinth in its center, of a wise man sitting cross-legged. I never knew who he was supposed to be. But some of the town's dreadlocked holy men—whom I now know as sadhus—bathed in its cool waters and forbade anyone else from doing so. I remembered once gashing my leg on a barbed-wire fence running away from them, after my brothers and I crept in on a really hot day. There were probably better ways to try to identify the place (who knew what might have been demolished since my time there?), but I hadn't really imagined what I'd do when I reached this stage. It now seems absurd, but I suppose I thought I'd find a town labeled "Ginestlay" and that would be that; I'd know I'd found home. But nothing else had worked out as I'd thought it would—this town was well outside my search boundary, and after all my careful planning and methodical efforts, I'd found it by accident. It seemed almost fitting that it should turn up this way—my destiny appeared to be riddled with close calls, chance episodes, and wonderful, blessed luck.

I went to bed for another restless night.

Mum and Dad's caution proved well-founded. When I woke the next day, I opened my computer first thing and saw that I'd received a response to my query about the fountain on the Khandwa Facebook page:

well we cant tell u exactly . . . there is a garden near cinema but the fountain is not that much big . . . the cinema is closed for years . . . we will try to update some pics . . . hope u will recollect something . . .

It was deflating, and I cursed myself for getting carried away and telling everyone too early. Why hadn't I waited to get word back from people who knew the place itself? But I tried to stay calm. Although this wasn't the confirmation I'd been hoping for, it wasn't a complete dismissal, either. I thanked the administrator and headed off to work in a mental fog. It was hard to concentrate as maps and memories swirled around in my mind. Could it all be wishful thinking? Had I been wasting my time?

Later that day, or perhaps it was the next, Mum told me she had looked at the map we'd drawn together in her notebook when I was six, and the configuration of the bridge, the river, and the train station weren't quite what I'd shown her on Google Earth—but was that because I had the wrong place, or because I'd had trouble drawing an accurate map as a six-year-old? She'd also pulled out the wall map I used to have in my bedroom—she kept everything to do with my brother's and my upbringing— and been surprised to find that it had both Burhanpur and Khandwa marked on it. To her they seemed so far away from Kolkata that she wondered whether it was possible I could have traveled that distance. It was almost all the way across an enormous country.

The first thing that hit me was that my home had been marked on the map above my desk the whole time, if I'd only known where to look. How many times had I looked at all those names, not knowing their secrets? I don't remember if I ever noticed Burhanpur among the several similar names on the map when I was younger; if I had, I'd obviously written it off, probably as being too far from Kolkata. And that was the second thing—it *was* much farther than I thought possible. Was it too far? Did the trains go much faster than everyone had allowed for? Or had I been on the train for longer than I thought?

Two surreal days passed. I was stuck between maps and memories. The things I'd always been so certain about were dissolving in the face of what I'd found. Were my greatest fears coming to fruition? Would the search erode what I thought I knew and leave me with nothing? My parents, Lisa, and I didn't talk much more about my breakthrough over the next couple of days, and I wondered whether they were being overly cautious or waiting for me to produce some solid evidence. It took me all that time, waiting for a second reply from the Khandwa group, to think to ask them the obvious question:

Can anyone tell me the name of the town or suburb on the top right hand side of Khandwa? i think it starts with G . . . not

sure how you spell it, but i think it goes like this (Ginestlay)?
The town is Muslim one side and Hindus on the other which
was 24 years ago but might be different now.

It took another day to get an answer. But when the answer came it was heart-stopping:

Ganesh Talai

That was as close to my childhood mispronunciation as you could hope for.

In my excitement, I called Mum and Dad immediately to tell them that now there could be no doubt. They remained worried but conceded that it all lined up. I had found Burhanpur and Khandwa and now, vitally, I had found Ganesh Talai, the area where I'd lived, where my Indian family might still be living, still wondering what had become of me.

In the immediate aftermath of my discovery, I wasn't sure what to do. I was overwhelmed. On the one hand, I was so excited to have succeeded that it was hard to think about anything else. But on the other, underneath these feelings was a faint nervous uncertainty, which meant for the time being that I kept the news among Lisa, my family, and me. What if I was wrong? What if

I was stirring everybody up on the basis of a mistake? What if I was making a fool of myself? I kept revisiting the streets of Khandwa on my laptop, probing them for more revelations and confirmations, almost paralyzed by the prospect of the truth. It was like when Mantosh and I were kids, too scared to go to India on the family trip. I was anxious, and the anxiety manifested itself as doubt.

From the moment I found my village, I tried to keep my expectations tempered. I tried to convince myself that my family couldn't possibly be there after all this time. How old would my mother be by now? I wondered. I wasn't sure, but she'd lived a hard life as a laborer in tough surroundings, so I didn't think that her life expectancy would be great. Was my sister, Shekila, okay? And Kallu? What had happened to Guddu that night in Burhanpur? Did he blame himself for my getting lost? Would any of them recognize me if we met again? Would I recognize them? How could you possibly find four people in all of India, when all you knew was where they lived a quarter of a century ago? Surely it was impossible.

My mind pinged back and forth between hope and denial, trying to find some way to feel settled with these new possibilities.

There was, of course, only one way to answer these questions. I wouldn't know that this was the right place for certain without going there. I would only know it if I saw it. And then, if I was completely convinced, I told myself, I would be happy just to take off my shoes and feel the earth beneath my feet, and remember the times when I used to walk the streets and paths. I couldn't let myself think further than that, about who might still be living there.

I knew my parents would worry about the prospect of my taking a trip to India. While I was much older than the child they'd planned to take on vacation, the same emotional and frightening feelings that made them cancel the last trip might still be stirred up. And if I discovered that it was the wrong place, what would that do to me? Would I stay there and search for the right one? Would I spiral into a pit of despair?

I spent some time researching Khandwa from half a world away. It's a small regional city of less than a quarter of a million people, in the Hindu-majority state of Madhya Pradesh—a quiet area well-known for its cotton, wheat, and soybean farming, as well as a major hydropower plant. My family was too poor to be involved in any of that industry, so all of this was news to me. Like most Indian cities, it has a long history and a list of Hindu saints attached to it, and it can boast a number of Bollywood stars who grew up there. Although it's not on the tourist trail, it is at a major rail junction, where the major east–west line between Mumbai and Kolkata meets another trunk route running from Delhi down to Goa and Kochi. That explains why Khandwa's station is much larger than the one at Burhanpur, although the towns are about the same size.

I watched the few clips of the town on YouTube, but it was hard to glean much from these images. Some footage showed the underpass near the railway station, apparently known as Teen Pulia, and the pedestrian overpass across the tracks, which appeared to have been extended over all three platforms. It still looked like home.

Some weeks passed in this way before I summoned the courage to raise the proposition of going to India. Even then, I edged around to it—I asked Mum and Dad what they would do in my situation. They said it was obvious: I had to go. Who wouldn't want to visit to make sure? Lisa felt the same way. And, of course, they all wanted to come with me.

I was relieved that they thought I had to go, and touched that they wanted to come to support me, but this was something that I needed to do alone.

I felt strongly about this for a number of reasons. Partly, I still worried about the possibility of being mistaken—what if we ended up standing in some backstreet, with Mum and Dad and Lisa staring at me as I was forced to admit I didn't know where we were? Also, I didn't want to make a big scene—a group of us descending on Ganesh Talai would probably draw lots of attention, and who knew what kinds of commotion that might cause? I could probably track down the phone number for the local police or the hospital in Ganesh Talai and call ahead to ask them about my family or to search for my medical records. I could provide my family's names at least and make some inquiries. It's not a big neighborhood, and everyone knows one another. But I feared that word would get out very quickly and opportunists would start appearing, making false claims. Some might well like the idea of a Western comparatively well-off prodigal son, and it wouldn't be surprising if a few potential "mothers" turned up at the station ready to claim their long-lost boy. By the time I got there, my preparations might make it harder to find my real family. Without any pre-announcements or entourage, I ought to be able to slip in relatively unnoticed and make my own judgments.

Moreover, I didn't know what to expect—possibly even dangerous situations in such an unpredictable country—and I didn't want to have to worry about everyone else or be distracted by them. Alone, I would just have the facts of my situation, and my own response to it, to deal with.

Maybe ultimately my reasoning was even simpler than that: this was my journey, and thus far I'd made it by myself, from the trains to the late nights on the Internet—it just felt right that I complete it alone.

Thankfully, Lisa said she understood. But my parents were more insistent. Dad promised that they would keep out of the way and let me do what I needed to do on my own. Or perhaps just he could come, for support and to help with any problems? He would stay in the hotel, but at least he'd be on hand. "I won't slow you down," he said. Although these were kind and well-meaning offers, my mind was already made up.

However, it was eleven months after I first identified Ganesh Talai before I stepped foot on the plane. Apart from my childhood flight to Australia, this was my first major trip anywhere, and in addition to the normal travel stuff, there were more than the usual administrative questions to resolve—even the matter of citizenship. When I had arrived from India, my passport showed that I was an Indian citizen. But it was not entirely accurate: it also stated that I was born in Calcutta, which, of course, was incorrect, but the Indian authorities couldn't very well leave the forms blank. Now I am an Australian citizen; my Indian citizenship had expired but it hadn't been officially canceled. Little bureaucratic details like these took time to work through.

Bureaucracy aside, though, the truth was that I was putting things off. I tried not to show it—and didn't even really acknowledge it to myself—but I was extremely anxious about the trip. Not only were there the questions of whether I'd found the right place and whether there'd be anyone there to reunite with; the prospect of returning to India also meant I had to face up to some bad memories. I wondered how I'd handle it.

Still, I booked my ticket, refused offers of company, and tried to prepare myself as best I could. Support came from unusual quarters. When I went to the medical clinic for the necessary vaccinations, my doctor asked the reason for my travel. Although I had generally kept my story to myself and close friends, now that I felt I'd found my home, I was less guarded about it, and for some reason I told him a little, and then a lot, about what was taking me to India. He was stunned and thanked me for sharing the incredible details. When I returned for follow-up vaccinations, others at the office had heard about my story, and I received a lot of attention from well-wishers. It was nice to feel that this other team was on my side in the weeks leading up to my departure, and it helped keep me in good spirits.

When the day finally came, Mum, Lisa, and I had a final cup of coffee together at the airport and once more went through the possible scenarios that awaited me. They told me to try to take it as it came, and not to get overwrought in terms of what I wanted to happen. Perhaps I hadn't done such a great job of disguising my anxiety, after all. Then Mum handed me a sheet of photos she had scanned from when I was a little boy. It had been twenty-five years since I'd been seen in India—even my own family might need help recognizing me. It was an extremely smart parting gift—I couldn't believe that with all my fretful preparations, I hadn't thought of it myself, but that probably reveals a lot about my state of mind at the time.

Even then, I lingered with final good-byes and was the last to board the plane. Mum looked at me nervously, and that triggered my own worries once more. Was I doing the right thing?

Did I really need to find out about the past when I had all of these people who loved me very much here with me now?

Yes. Of course, the answer was yes. I had to find out where I was from, if I could, even if only to put it behind me. I wanted to at least see the place I had been dreaming about for decades.

I got on the plane.

10.

Meeting My Mother

When I landed on February 11, 2012, in the city of Indore, the biggest city in Madhya Pradesh, my feet touched the ground in India for the first time since I'd left as a child. In the predawn dark, I felt a rush of adrenaline as the magnitude of this journey hit me.

India didn't exactly welcome me back. My first experiences firmly established me as a stranger—I might have come "home," but this was a country foreign to me. My bag was missing from the luggage-claim carousel. When I tried to ask an airport official where it might be, he replied in what I think was Hindi and I didn't understand a word. The official soon went to fetch someone who spoke some English. It seems a little thing not to speak the language, but it carried extra weight for a man making an emotional journey home after years of being lost. It was like being lost all over again, unable to understand what anyone said or to make people understand me.

I made a mess of negotiating my way out of several insistent but exorbitant offers of a taxi to the hotel where I was staying overnight before going on to Khandwa, and I eventually found the courtesy bus. The sun blazed into life as the bus pulled out of the airport, and I got my first look at the pressing confusion of twenty-first-century India.

At first much of it looked like the India I had known a quarter of a century earlier. I saw black wild pigs scavenging in side streets, recognizable trees on street corners, and the familiar press of people everywhere. The poverty was still evident, but I was quickly struck by how much dirtier everything appeared from how I remembered it. People were relieving themselves on the roadside and there was rubbish strewn everywhere—I didn't remember the same things from my own neighborhood, but maybe I'd become accustomed to the clean, open spaces of Hobart.

When I stepped off the bus at the hotel, the unrelenting noise of heavy traffic and the strong smell of sulfur, from drains and sewerage, hit my senses. I realized that after such a long time, Khandwa would probably seem different, too. I was exhausted and decided to try to rest a bit before trying to find a driver to take me to Khandwa. After a fitful few hours' sleep, I organized a car and driver who said he would take me there the next day.

Khandwa was two hours away, and I paid half of what the drivers at the airport had quoted me for the few kilometers' ride to the hotel. But perhaps you paid extra for safety: my short, skinny driver took to the roads like a maniac (even by the famously carefree standards of India), which added another shot of adrenaline to my overloaded system. The road from Indore runs through hills and valleys, but I noticed little of the scenery. We stopped occasionally for a chai and a cigarette, and I found myself growing more and more anxious about what awaited me in Khandwa. The death-defying trip couldn't go quickly enough.

Under a hot sun in clear skies, we approached the outskirts of town. I didn't recognize the place at all, which gave me an instant chill. The area had a dusty gray industrial look that I wasn't familiar with. Suddenly, I decided to go straight to the railway station before the hotel—I was past dragging things out, and that would be the quickest and easiest way to discover whether what I had worked out on my laptop back at home in Tasmania was right. We changed direction.

The roads were narrow and traffic slowed to a crawl—it was Sunday and people were out and about everywhere. When I was little, there had been more horses and carts than auto-rickshaws, but now the streets were clogged with cars and motorbikes.

My mobile phone had a GPS service, which would have laid out a street map for me, but my battery was low and I wanted my memory to be jolted into service. So I directed the driver to the best of my memory, and, sure enough, we found the station where I expected it to be. My spirits lifted.

The station looked a little different from how I remembered it, but I found that I instantly had my bearings—from this point, I could find my way to anywhere in Khandwa. I knew where I was . . . and I wasn't far from home.

At that point, exhaustion overwhelmed me. I felt like a puppet with his strings cut. Since I'd arrived in India—and for a long while before that—I had been running on nervous energy, but now that I knew I was in the right place, I was drained. I asked the driver to take me to the hotel—I'd walk the streets the next day.

As the taxi crawled through the streets of Khandwa, I tested them against my memory. I remembered the place being green, with trees everywhere, less industrialized and polluted, and certainly with no garbage in the streets. The buildings looked much shabbier than I had pictured them. But when we drove through an underpass beneath the train tracks with barely any overhead clearance, memories of just such a claustrophobic road came flooding back. It was surely the one where I had played as a child.

At the Hotel Grand Barrack—as the name suggests, it was once a British army barracks—I inadvertently offended my driver by offering no *baksheesh*, or tip. From being in Australia, I simply wasn't used to paying more than the agreed amount, and I walked inside the hotel before I realized my mistake. I checked in, feeling like I was carrying around a culture clash.

Exhausted by my discoveries and the lengthy travel, I put my suitcase down in my hotel room, switched on the air-conditioning and overhead fan, and collapsed on the bed.

But tired as I was, I couldn't settle. Perhaps I was over-wrought, but I thought: *What the heck am I doing? I've been sitting on planes for an eternity, squashed in a car for two hours more. . . . Get going!* It was Sunday, two o'clock; I had come a long way to find my home. I grabbed my daypack and water bottle, and felt a surge of excitement.

Standing outside the hotel, I didn't know which way to go first—roads and lanes led off in every direction—so I retraced the route the car had taken. Soon I was walking on the road parallel to the railway line, striding back toward the center of town.

Despite a certain familiarity with the streets, I couldn't quite say that I knew precisely where I was. So much was different, I just couldn't be sure. Doubts began to creep back into my mind—after all, how different could railway stations and underpasses look in Indian towns and cities, and how many towns and cities were there? Might I have made a mistake? But my feet seemed to know the way, as though I was on automatic, and jet lag, fatigue, and the surreal nature of the experience made me feel like I was observing my progress from outside myself. I was failing to take Mum's advice to remain calm and keep my expectations low. Instinct, memory, doubt, and excitement were all coursing through me at once.

After a while, I came upon a small green mosque—Baba, the holy man's mosque. I had forgotten all about it! It looked similar to what I now remembered; more run-down and of course smaller, but the resemblance was still reassuring. I began to feel again that I was on the right track. But I still relentlessly questioned everything I saw: *Did it look like that? Is this mission right? Am I going the right way?*

A bit farther up the road, my instinct told me to turn left, to head toward the center of Ganesh Talai. I began to tremble and my pace slowed. This didn't look right at all. There were too many houses; it was too built up. I tried to calm myself down—things change, populations grow. Of course it was more crowded. But if old buildings had been knocked down for new ones, maybe my house was gone, too! That made me shudder, and I hurried on until I came to a small section of open ground that looked like a spot where I used to play.

At once I both could and could not recognize the spot. It was the same place but different. Then I realized what the difference was: the town now had electricity. There were poles and wires everywhere. When I was growing up, our house was lit with candles and we cooked on a wood stove or with kerosene. Now that the streets were draped with electricity cables, the whole place looked more closed in, busier, transformed.

I had worked myself up into a state, less, I suspect, about identifying the place and the buildings and more about what else might have changed. Up until this point, I'd deliberately put my mother and family in the back of my mind as best I could. Now I was approaching where they might still be. Despite my best efforts, all sorts of emotions were bubbling to the surface. I decided to start by trying to find the first house my family had lived in while we were still living in the Hindu neighborhood.

Making my way down a street and into a narrow, twisting alleyway, I saw a woman at its end washing clothes. As I looked down the alley, memories of running around the place flooded through me. I must have been staring, because the woman spoke to me—a strange man in casual Western sportswear, probably rich-looking to her, certainly appearing out of place. I think she said something like "Can I help you?" in Hindi, but all I knew to respond with was "No." I turned and walked on.

I could no longer delay the inevitable. It was time to face the ultimate point of my journey. It only took a few minutes to walk across the few streets that once separated the Hindu and Muslim areas of the neighborhood. My heart was in my mouth as I approached the place where I remembered the crumbling brick flat to be. And before I could think about what I was expecting, I found myself standing right in front of it.

It looked so tiny to me, but it was unmistakable.

It was also unmistakably abandoned.

I stood and stared.

The rough brick walls were familiar, though the ground level was now plastered with cheap concrete and whitewashed. The doorway to the corner room was in exactly the right place, but the door itself was broken. It was the size of an Australian window. I couldn't see much through the cracks in the door, so around the corner I peered in through the sole window, barely thirty centimeters square. I couldn't believe that my entire family of five—though not always at once—had occupied the tiny, dark space inside. It was perhaps three meters, or nine feet, square. The little fireplace was still there, clearly not used for some time, but the clay water tank was gone. The single shelf was hanging off its brackets. Some of the outer wall's bricks had fallen away, letting in beams of light. The cowpat-and-mud floor, which my mother had always kept clean swept, was now dusty from disuse.

While I looked in, a goat chewed at some hay left on a rock by the door, indifferent to my personal ordeal. Although I'd told myself over and over that I couldn't expect to just fly to India and find my family safe and well in the same place after all this time, it was hard to absorb that I'd found the flat but it was completely empty. Secretly, I had been convinced that if I found my way back home, they'd be here waiting. In a daze, completely hollowed out with disappointment, I watched the goat eat.

I had no idea what to do next. My search was over.

As I stood there with no further plan in mind, a young Indian woman holding a baby came out of the next door. She spoke to me in Hindi, and I understood that she was asking if she could help me. I replied, "I don't speak Hindi, I speak English." I was jolted out of my slump when she said, "I speak English, a little." Quickly I said, "This house . . ." and then recited the names of my family: "Kamla, Guddu, Kallu, Shekila, Saroo." The woman didn't respond, so I repeated the names and pulled out the sheet of photos Mum had given me before I left. That was when she told me what I couldn't bear to hear: no one lived here anymore.

It was then that two men walked over to see what was happening, and it was the second—perhaps in his midthirties, and with good English—who listened as I told my story, looked as I pointed at the photos and then at myself. He told me to wait, and then walked off down an alley. I didn't have much time to think about what was happening—other people had begun gathering near us, curious as to what was going on and about the presence of a foreigner in these streets where tourists never visit.

After a couple of minutes, the man returned and said words I'll never forget: "Come with me. I'm going to take you to your mother."

He said it very directly, like an official making an announcement, so bluntly that I just accepted it. I didn't absorb what he'd said until I'd begun to do as he'd asked and followed him down an adjacent alley. Then I got goose bumps and my head began to spin—just moments ago I'd given up on twenty-five years of hoping for exactly this moment. Could it possibly be true that this passing stranger knew where my mother was? It seemed too unlikely and too fast.

After all this time, things were moving at a bewildering pace.

When we had walked about fifteen meters, the man stopped in front of three women who were standing outside a doorway, all of them now looking in my direction. "This is your mother," he said.

I was too stunned to ask which one—I half wondered whether this was a prank.

Incapable of doing anything else, I looked from one to the next. The first was certainly not her. There was something familiar about the woman in the middle, and the third woman was a stranger. It had to be the woman in the middle. She was slender and seemed so small, with graying hair pulled back in a bun, and wearing a bright yellow floral dress.

Despite the years, I knew the fine bone structure of her face the instant I looked back at her, and in that moment she seemed to know me, too.

We looked at each other for a second longer, and I felt a sharp stab of grief that it could take a mother and son even a few moments to simply recognize each other, and then a rush of joy that we now had. She stepped forward, took my hands, and held them, and stared into my face with utter wonderment. I was thinking clearly enough in this moment to understand that whatever turmoil I had been experiencing on this journey, at least I'd had some chance to prepare. For my mother, her son had simply reappeared twenty-five years after she'd lost him.

Before either of us uttered a word, my mother took my hand and led me to her house. A long line of people followed, curious to see what was happening with the strange foreigner. Her house was only a hundred meters around the corner. As we walked, she seemed overcome with emotion. She muttered to herself in Hindi, then looked up at me again and again, with tears of joy in her eyes. I was too overwhelmed to say anything.

My mother's house, another conjoined dwelling of crumbling brick, was down a dirt alley, and she hustled me inside and sat me down on a bed in the main room. She remained standing and produced a mobile phone from within the layers of her clothing. When I heard her say, "Kallu, Shekila . . ." I understood that she was calling my siblings. They were still here, too? She spoke excitedly on the phone, screaming and laughing, and calling out, "Sheru! Sheru!" It took me a moment to realize that my mother was saying my name.

I was stunned. Was it possible I'd been mispronouncing my own name all this time?

The little knot of people that had assembled outside was growing rapidly, and soon there was quite a crowd. They were chatting excitedly to one another and into mobile phones—the miracle of the son returned from the dead was clearly big news, and word was being spread. The house was soon filled with boisterous, celebrating people, with more crowded in the alley outside the front door and even more gathered on the adjoining street.

Fortunately, some of these well-wishers spoke a little English, and my mother and I were finally able to talk through translators. The first thing she asked me was "Where have you been?" It would be a little while before I could give her an expansive answer, but I provided a quick sketch of how I came to be lost in Kolkata and adopted in Australia. Not surprisingly, she was astonished.

My mother told me that the man I had spoken to in the street had come to the house she was visiting and simply said to her, "Sheru is back." Then he had shown her the sheet of paper with the photographs on it that Mum had given me—which I don't even remember him taking—and said, "This boy who is now grown into a man is nearby and asking about Kamla, which is you." That seemed a strange thing to say, but I learned that my mother had converted to Islam many years earlier and had taken the new name Fatima. I think she will always be Kamla to me.

My mother described her reactions better than I ever could mine: she said she was "surprised with thunder" that her boy had come back, and that the happiness in her heart was "as deep as the sea."

When she had seen the photos, she had started shivering and ran from the house into the alley, where she was joined by the two women she had been visiting, and that was where they were when I appeared at the top of the alleyway.

She said that as I walked toward her she had still been shaking and felt cold, with "the thunder in her head" as joyful tears welled in her eyes.

I had thunder in my head, too. And after all the slowness of travel and the quiet yet highly emotional ups and downs of walking the streets of Ganesh Talai to our old flat, now everything was happening in a mad, chaotic rush. There were people shouting and laughing everywhere, pressing in to get a look at me, a babble of Hindi I couldn't understand, and my mother smiling and crying. It was too much to comprehend.

Later I realized that I had been just fifteen meters away from her, literally around the corner, when I turned up in front of our old home, but if that man had not come along and helped me, I might have walked away. I probably would have found her in the end, after asking around more, but I'm haunted by the possibility that I might not have, that we might have stood so near to each other and never known.

We were really only able to talk in fits and starts, what with all the hubbub as messages were translated, and people asked questions, and the story was repeated for the benefit of newcomers. My mother would turn to her friends, grinning widely, then simply look at me or hug me with tears on her face. Then she'd get on the phone again to spread the word to more people.

There were a lot of questions to be answered, of course. My mother had no idea what had happened to me since the night I disappeared. With so much to fill her in on, it was slow work, but luckily we had the help of an unlikely interpreter, a woman who lived a few doors away, called Cheryl, whose father was British and whose mother was Indian.

I was so grateful to have Cheryl's help; with it by degrees I managed to make myself understood to my mother. Later I would be able to tell her everything, but at that first reunion I could only cut through the chaos with the basics: being trapped on a train, ending up in Calcutta, and being adopted and growing up in Australia. That I had come back after so many years was astonishing to my mother; that I'd come from somewhere as far away as Australia was incomprehensible.

Even at this first meeting, she told me she was grateful to my parents who had raised me in Australia, and that they had the right to call me their son because they had raised me from a child and made me the man I was today. Her only concern for me, she said, was that I should have the very best life I could. It was extremely moving to hear her say these words. She didn't realize it, but her words took me back to being a little boy at the

Nava Jeevan orphanage, deciding whether to accept the Brierleys' offer of adoption. She allowed me to feel, without reservation, that I'd made the right decision. She also said she was proud of me, which is all anyone can wish to hear from his mother.

The run-down building my mother now lived in was, in some ways, even more dilapidated than our old abandoned home. The bricks in the front wall were crumbling, leaving obvious gaps. In the front room of about two by three meters, where she slept on the single bed on which she had me seated, two pieces of corrugated iron came down from the roof to a junction, obviously to channel rainwater into a bowl in the small adjacent bathroom, with its squat toilet and tub of water for washing. It disturbed me to see that the way it was built also meant that rain could just blow inside. There was a slightly larger room at the back, serving as a kitchen. But although it was far too small for all the curious people who were trying to get inside, her home was larger than our old place, and at least it had a terrazzo floor rather than compacted dirt. It was in shocking condition, but in the context of Ganesh Talai, it represented a step up, and I knew she would have had to work hard for that. I learned from others that my mother was too old to carry stones on her head on building sites anymore, and so she now worked as a housecleaner. Despite the hardship of her life, she said that she was happy.

Over the next couple of hours, people continued to arrive, crowding around the barred window and doorway, excitedly chatting and being filled in on the gossip. My mother held court for many groups of visitors, sitting next to me and holding my face or hugging me while she talked, or leaping up to answer the phone, now ringing off the hook.

Finally, two special guests were ushered inside in quick succession—my brother Kallu and sister, Shekila. When Shekila arrived, with her husband and two sons, our mother was holding me and crying, and my sister burst into tears as I stood to embrace her. Kallu then arrived alone on a motorbike and was stunned to lay eyes on me. We instantly recognized each other, but each of us was seeing his brother as an adult for the first time. Neither of my siblings had had any cause to learn English, so this was another reunion of tears, smiles, and speechless wonder before Cheryl's assistance with some simple communication. It was bittersweet to be so close to my family and yet still cut off in this fundamental way.

I had one final pressing question: where was Guddu? Of all the stories I wanted to hear, his was at the top of the list. What had happened that night in Burhanpur? Was it something he thought about often? Above all, I wanted him to know that I didn't blame him for anything—I was sure it was an accident, and I'd never stopped looking for him. Now I had finally found my way back.

That's when I was told the hardest news I'd ever hear. When I asked my mother about him, she replied sadly, "He is no longer."

Guddu had also never returned that night I was lost. My mother found out a few weeks later that he had died in a train accident at age fourteen. She had lost two sons on the same night. I couldn't imagine how she had borne it.

If there was one thing more I could have wished for from that visit, it was to see Guddu again, even if only once. It was because I'd missed him so much that I made him take me to Burhanpur. To hear that he had died was devastating.

Later I learned more about that evening and what my mother thought had happened to us both. At first she was a little annoyed that I'd gone off with Guddu because I was needed to look after Shekila. But the India I began life in was not like Australia, where a child missing for an hour can cause alarm—my mother was herself often gone for days, and even young children might be in and out of the house unsupervised. So initially she wasn't too concerned. But after a week had passed, she began to worry. It wasn't unusual for Guddu to be away for weeks, but it was irresponsible of him to keep me away for this long. Kallu hadn't seen us on his travels and didn't know whether we'd been around Burhanpur, and my mother started to fear the worst. She had Kallu ask around Khandwa and Burhanpur if anyone had seen us, but they heard nothing.

A few weeks, possibly a month, after our disappearance, a

policeman came to the house. More worried about me, being the youngest and least capable, my mother thought he had come with bad news of where I was, but he hadn't—he had come about Guddu. He said that Guddu had died in a railway accident and showed her a photo of his body. Guddu was found by the tracks about a kilometer outside Burhanpur, and the policeman was there to ask her to formally identify him. I asked if she had been sure it was him, and she nodded slowly. It was still a very painful subject for her, so I got the rest of the details from Kallu. Guddu had somehow fallen from a moving train and either went under a wheel or struck something fixed by the side of the track. Half of one of his arms had been severed and he had lost one of his eyes—an unimaginably horrific thing for a mother to have to look at.

I wanted to visit Guddu's grave, but my family told me that wasn't possible—houses had been built over the graveyard he was in, and the builders hadn't even bothered to move the remains of the dead before they began construction. The owners or developers either didn't want to know or didn't care. It wasn't easy to hear. I felt as if my brother had been taken from me, just as I had been taken from him—disappeared without a trace—and in a corner of my mind I understood a little more of what my family must have felt about my vanishing. We didn't even have any photographs of Guddu, as we could never afford family portraits. He had been part of us as we had been part of him, and now all that remained of Guddu were our memories.

I wasn't sure if my family entirely understood why I was so upset about not having a grave to sit by. For them, Guddu's death was long in the past, but for me his death happened suddenly that very day. Not being able to properly grieve for my departed brother was a deep-seated loss that I felt strongly long after I returned to Australia. The last thing he had said to me on that platform in Burhanpur was that he would be back. Perhaps he'd never returned; perhaps he'd come back to find me gone. Either way, I'd hoped to be able to be reunited with him. Now I'll never know what happened that night—some of our mysteries will never be solved.

My family was now experiencing nearly the opposite. Rather than grieving a sudden, unexpected death, they were rejoicing in a sudden, unexpected, seemingly miraculous homecoming. All of these years, they feared that the two brothers had suffered the same fate, or something worse had happened to me. I felt for Kallu particularly: he lost two brothers and suddenly became the eldest male, a charge that came with great responsibility in our community. He would have been seen as equally responsible for the family's welfare as my mother, a huge weight on his young, bereft shoulders.

I also learned a little about my father. He was still alive but no longer lived in Khandwa; he'd moved with his second family to Bhopal, the capital of Madhya Pradesh, a couple of hundred kilometers to the north—the city that was made famous by a chemical disaster at the Union Carbide plant in the early eight-ies. The family still hated him for abandoning us, so my curiosity about him would have to wait.

Amid all the chaos and celebration that day, Cheryl men-tioned to me that some of the people there were asking my mother how she could be sure I was her son. Wasn't it possible that I was an imposter, or that we were both mistaken, swept away in events because we so wanted them to be true? My mother answered that a mother knows her child anywhere—she'd had no doubt I was who I said I was from the first moment she saw me. But there was one way to be completely sure. She held my head in her hands and tilted it, looking for the scar above my eye from when I fell in the street, running away from a dog. There it was, on the right side, just above the brow. She pointed to it and smiled—indeed, I was her son.

My mother's house was full of well-wishers late into the eve-ning. Eventually, I had to go—I was completely sapped, and my head and heart were so full, they felt like they were about to burst. It took a long while to say good-bye to everyone, even without many words in common—there were lots of long looks and hugs. I suppose at the back of everyone's mind was the ques-tion of whether I'd come back after I walked out the door this time. I promised that I would, the next day. Finally, my mother let me go, and watched as I climbed behind Kallu on his motorbike and sped off. I thanked him as I got off at the Grand Barrack, and he left for the hour's ride back to Burhanpur—the town I'd spent so long trying to find—where, ironically, he now lived.

Back in my room, I thought about how my life had completely changed since earlier that afternoon. I had found my family. I was no longer an orphan. And the search that had meant so much to me for so long was over. I wondered what I was going to do now.

I thought a lot about Guddu. It was hard to imagine what might have happened to him. Guddu was so confident navigating trains, having worked on them for so long, that I couldn't believe he simply fell. There had to be another explanation. Perhaps he had returned to discover me gone and went looking for me. There were kids my brothers had run-ins with from time to time—maybe he'd got it into his head that they had done something to me and started a fight? The worst possibility was that he might have felt guilty about leaving me alone, and in his panic to find me had taken risks or been preoccupied, and that was the reason he'd fallen.

He might have assumed I'd gone home, but he never went back to check, so it was hard not to think that if I hadn't boarded the train that night, Guddu might have returned as planned and he'd still be alive now. Intellectually, I knew I couldn't accept responsibility for his fate, but it was a dark thought that was hard to shake. And although I usually felt there was an answer for everything, that you just needed to work at a problem until you solved it, this time I understood that I would have to accept I could never know the truth of what had happened to my brother.

Before getting into bed, I sent a text to Mum and Dad at home in Hobart:

The questions I wanted answered have been answered. There are no more dead ends. My family is true and genuine, as we are in Australia. My mother has thanked you, mum and dad, for bringing me up. She and my brother and sister understand that you and dad are my family, and they don't want to intervene in any way. They are happy just knowing that I'm alive, and that's all they want. I hope you know that you guys are first with me, which will never change. Love you.

Not surprisingly, sleep was difficult.

11.

Reconnection

Kallu picked me up on his motorbike early the next morning and took me back to our mother's house. She greeted me almost as enthusiastically as she had the day before; perhaps she really hadn't believed that I would come back.

Kallu had already delivered his wife, son, and daughter to the house before coming back for me, and he presented them to me—incredibly, all four had made the trip from Burhanpur on the motorbike. I had been delighted the day before to discover I was an uncle to Shekila's two sons, and I loved meeting my niece and third nephew.

There was a brief moment of quiet as we all had tea, smiling at each other, but before long the tumult was on again, as we exchanged stories with help from Cheryl and other translators, and greeted endless visitors—and that was how it was to be for the next four days. Shekila soon joined us with her husband and children, having again made the two-hour journey from her home in Harda, a hundred kilometers to the northeast.

My family inevitably asked me about my wife and kids. It surprised them that I didn't have any. I suppose by this age I'd have a family, too, if I'd grown up in India. But they seemed pleased to hear that I had a girlfriend at least, although I wasn't entirely convinced that my mother understood the concept.

By that second day, the local news media had heard about the lost boy who had suddenly rematerialized as a man in the streets of Ganesh Talai. They were soon joined by the national media, who arrived bristling with TV cameras. Their questioning—mostly through translators—was relentless, and as I told my story over and over again, it began to feel as though it had happened to someone else.

The media interest came as a genuine surprise. It hadn't crossed my mind that my return would cause such a fuss, and I wasn't remotely ready for it. It made an emotionally demanding situation even more so, but I found something wonderful in it, too. There are more than a billion people in India, and there are kids roaming the streets with no one to care for them. It can seem a chaotic, even harsh, place. Yet here in Ganesh Talai—in fact, around the whole country—people could get wildly excited because just one of those lost children had managed to reconnect with his family after an incredibly long time apart.

As more people came flocking to see me, the gathering turned into a public celebration, with music and people dancing in the streets. I was moved by their reaction and also shaken by the entire turn of events; my emotions were almost overwhelming to me. My return seemed to inspire and energize the neighborhood, as though it was evidence that the hard luck of life did not have to rule you. Sometimes miracles do happen.

My family seems to be one that holds in our emotions until they build up such pressure that we have no choice but to release them. When we had some time to ourselves, we all wept a lot, from happiness but also from the sadness of the time we'd lost. I was now thirty, Kallu, thirty-three, and Shekila, twenty-seven. I had last seen Shekila as a tiny child whom I'd had to keep watch over, and now she had two beautiful children of her own.

I remembered something and grabbed a bit of charcoal from the fireplace, showing her. She laughed, recalling the times when she used to eat it as a baby. The fact that we could laugh about it now showed how far we had come from those days.

Shekila and Kallu were lucky enough to have gone to school. With Guddu and me gone, our mother had just been able to afford to send them. Shekila had become a schoolteacher, able to speak and write Hindi and Urdu (but not English). Shekila told me that when she got the call from our mother the day before, she didn't believe it—she'd thought it might be someone pulling a scam or playing a joke. But my mother's conviction, and especially her description of the sheet of photos of me as a kid, brought Shekila around. She had thanked God for the miracle and quickly got on a train to join us. She said that when she had laid eyes on me again, she had been "lost in time," taken back to the days when I looked after her. She had known it was me straightaway.

Kallu had also done well for himself. He was now a factory manager, with a supplementary income as a school bus driver. So in one generation, my family's occupations went from stone-carrying laborer to teacher and manager. It seems a bittersweet result of the family's loss that the remaining children had managed to lift themselves out of poverty. But life hadn't been easy for Kallu—I was deeply saddened to hear that I'd been right about his life after Guddu and I disappeared.

The burden of being the only man in the house had weighed on him heavily. Although he had been sent to school after my disappearance, he had cut his schooling short in order to learn to drive so he could get better work to try to support Shekila and our mother. The pain of loss had never left him, and it eventually caused him to leave Ganesh Talai and Khandwa altogether and move to Burhanpur. He told me that he'd even questioned his Hindu faith at times but had felt that the gods would "do justice" one day and I would return. My return affected him deeply. Perhaps it would mean that some of the wounds he had carried for so long could begin to heal and his burdens could be shared.

We talked more about the difficult times my family had endured after my disappearance—Shekila even admitted to being scared about sending her little kids to school in case one day they didn't come back. But there was laughter, too, of course. One thing that left me bemused was the discovery that I was christened Sheru, Hindi for "lion." I'd mispronounced my name ever since I became lost—and now I'd forever be Saroo.

I found that being in Ganesh Talai brought back a lot of memories about my life there, and talking with my family brought back even more, most of which I'd been too young to understand at the time. The things I learned that day, and in the couple of days that followed, helped me to fill in some of the gaps in the picture of my early life—a life that's ordinary for millions of small-town Indians. Our conversations also helped me understand the life my birth mother had led; her resilience in the face of its harshness made me admire her even more.

My mother's family was of the Rajput warrior caste, and her father was a policeman. She was named Kamla after the Hindu goddess of creation, Kamala. I remembered her as having been beautiful, and I still found her so, despite the passage of so many backbreaking and often heartbreaking years.

My father had worked as a building contractor. He was twenty-four and my mother eighteen when they married.

I've now learned much more about why I rarely saw my father. When I was around three (Guddu, nine, and Kallu, six), and my mother was pregnant with Shekila, my father announced he had taken another wife—which he was permitted to do as a Muslim—and was leaving us to live with her. My mother had apparently known nothing of my father's intention to marry again until he announced that he'd done so—a rude shock. My father had met his new wife at one of his building sites, where she was a laborer, hefting bricks and stones, and transporting them around on trays on her head. My mother would still see my father at times where he lived on the town's outskirts. His second wife was very jealous of her and would tell her off when they saw one another. My mother was convinced it was the new wife who prevented my father from seeing us. I certainly can't remember him visiting us at home.

My mother decided against seeking a divorce, although she could have done so under Islamic law, having been abandoned by her husband. She remained married to my father even though he no longer lived with or supported her.

She was deeply disturbed by all that had happened and described that terrible time as a hurricane tearing through her life. She described sometimes feeling so disoriented that she didn't know where the sky ended and the ground began. She wished to die—she even contemplated having us all take poison or lie down on the nearby railway line to be killed by the first passing train.

It was then that she decided to move us to the Muslim part of Ganesh Talai, to the flat that now lay unoccupied. She felt her Hindu family wouldn't take her back in, but the Muslim community seemed supportive of her despite her circumstances. I suspect she also felt that their more prosperous neighborhood was a better environment for her children to grow up in. I now found that the religious segregation I remembered had since been relaxed, and there were no longer clearly distinguished areas. Despite the move, my mother didn't formally convert to Islam until after my disappearance, although she didn't veil her face as some of her friends who visited did.

Now that I had found my mother, Kallu, and Shekila, the thought occurred to me that I might also seek out my father. Perhaps because I'd been away for so long, I thought I was open to the idea of seeing him again. It might be hard to imagine why, with so few memories of him and none very favorable. But he was a part of my identity, part of the story of my life. And perhaps sometimes families ought to offer forgiveness to people who wronged them in the past. However, with him some distance away, and my not knowing if he would want to see me anyway, I decided it wouldn't happen on this particular trip. I didn't mention these thoughts to anyone at the time, and as it was something I'd only want to do with their blessing, I knew

I'd have to raise the subject carefully when I had become re-acquainted with them. That visit with my father has not happened yet, but perhaps at some point it will.

As I spent more time with my family and reconnected with the place where I'd been born, I thought about the word everyone kept using, including me—"home." Was that where I was now, or was it where I'd come from?

I didn't know. After being lost, I'd been lucky enough to be adopted by a loving family, and I not only lived somewhere else, but had become someone other than the person I might have been had I stayed in India. I didn't just live in Australia; I thought of myself as an Australian. I had a family home with the Brierleys and had made my own home in Hobart with my girl-friend, Lisa. I knew I belonged, and was loved, in those places.

But finding Khandwa and my Indian family also felt like coming home. Something about being in the place just felt right. I was loved here, too, and belonged in a way I'd not thought much about beforehand and found hard to explain now. This was where I'd spent my first years, where my blood was.

So when it was time for me to return to Hobart—a time that came around far too quickly—I felt very deeply the wrench of leaving. I promised my mother, sister, and brother, and their young families, that I would be back soon. I had come to see that

I had two homes, each with its own emotional connections, even if they were thousands of kilometers apart.

This journey, which I'd embarked upon to resolve questions about who I was, was far from finished. I had some answers—lots of answers—but I also had a lot more questions. One thing was obvious: the trip between India and Australia—between my homes—was one I was destined to make many times.

12.

———

Reaching Out

While in India, I had received an excited text of congratulations from Asra, my old friend from Nava Jeevan, who had heard the news of my family reunion through our parents. Our families had remained close since our arrival in Melbourne all those years ago. When I got back to Hobart, I called her to share some of the joy of my experiences, mindful that she was orphaned by the death of her Indian parents and, sadly, would never be able to make the same journey. Asra was very happy for me, and asked what I was going to do now that I'd succeeded in reconnecting with my past. It had been such a whirlwind of revelations and emotions since I returned to Khandwa, I didn't know what to say.

I hadn't imagined anything much beyond finding my home and, maybe, my mother. I suppose I'd thought of that as the end of the story, but it was truly more like a new beginning. I now had two families, and I had to work out how I fit in with each of them—across the world and across cultures.

My parents and Lisa were relieved to have me back. Even though we'd spoken on the phone every day I was in India, they were worried there were things I wasn't telling them. At first they thought I might disappear again. Lisa kept worrying about my safety—I was in one of the poorer parts of a strange country, and who knew what to expect? I only fully realized when I got back how nerve-racking it had been for them.

That was soon forgotten, though, as everyone was anxious to hear about my meeting my family. They knew the main facts, of course, but now wanted all the details—what stories we had told each other, what the others had remembered of my childhood that I hadn't . . . and whether I wanted to return.

They seemed to be trying to work out whether I still wanted to be here or was thinking of moving to India. I reassured them as much as I could that although the experience had changed me in important ways, I was still the same Saroo. In reality, it took me a while to feel like my old self again, and to look at Hobart through my old eyes rather than those of a poor Indian.

There was one change that quickly became apparent: I was now someone with a story to tell, and lots of people wanted to hear it. The Hobart newspaper, *The Mercury*, contacted me soon after I returned. A reporter had got wind of the story somehow and I agreed to be interviewed about it. That opened the floodgates. After *The Age* in Melbourne and the *Sydney Morning Herald* came the international media.

We weren't prepared for my newfound celebrity—perhaps nobody can be. Sometimes the phone rang in the middle of the night as reporters called up from all over the world. Realizing that I needed help dealing with this attention, I got a manager. Soon book publishers and film producers were calling with offers. It was surreal. I'm a salesman for industrial pipes, hoses, and fittings; I was looking for my hometown and my family—not the limelight! While I enjoyed telling my story, it never occurred to me that I'd be a person with a manager who has to schedule media engagements. Fortunately, Lisa and my parents were very supportive and gave me all the time I needed. And even though it was exhausting to go over my story again and again with the media, I thought I had a kind of duty to do it, because it might help people—what had happened to me was remarkable, and might offer hope to others who wanted to find their lost family but thought it impossible. Perhaps people in different situations could also be inspired by my experience of grasping opportunities, no matter how daunting, and never giving up.

During this time, I stayed in touch with my Indian family via online videoconferencing, which they could access with a computer at a friend's house. Or at least they could partly access it—they didn't have a video camera at their end, so I couldn't see them, but they could see me and we could talk, either in our stilted way or through a translator. I decided I'd have to set my mother up so that we could stay in touch and see each other from across the world. Now that the family had finally been reunited, I wanted to play a proper part in it, building our connection and helping to look after my mother, sister, and brother, and my niece and nephews.

There were still many things I wanted to know, and I hoped they would become clearer when I returned to India for my second visit. It was almost winter, although the weather was still warm and the air was a choking smog. With weather like this, the sky is an orange-gray, and it doesn't change much as day turns to night.

I was heading to Khandwa in time for the end of Diwali, the Hindu "Festival of Lights." I had forgotten nearly everything about Indian culture, but Indians love festive occasions, so I knew it would be colorful. Diwali is a celebration of all things good and a rejection of evil. Lakshmi, the goddess of prosperity, is invoked and praised, and families display their wealth before her image in their household shrine and give thanks for their good fortune. There's feasting and gift giving, and traditionally little oil lamps are lit throughout people's homes and buildings are covered with colored lights, like in Australia during Christmas. There are also a lot of firecrackers, and I heard loud bangs all day, as people set them off to drive away evil spirits. At night the sky was lit up by fireworks.

I arrived as evening was settling, reaching the narrow streets of the old part of town as it was in the full swing of the festivities. My mother had told me I was always welcome to stay with her, but I knew she understood that I lived as a Westerner now and needed space and amenities her tiny flat couldn't provide. I thanked her for her generosity but told her it would be better for me to make use of the hotel, which wasn't far away, and visit her daily. So I had dropped my bags at the Hotel Grand Barrack and then had the taxi driver take me to join her and my family in Ganesh Talai.

We drove through the railway underpass, the streets alive with people out shopping, and the driver dropped me off in the square near Ganesh Talai's temple and mosque—located tolerantly close to each other. I set off on foot down the alleys of my childhood, feeling a little more at home.

I had been trying to learn Hindi before I returned, and I'd made some progress, but once I was in any sort of conversation, I was all at sea. (I've heard there is a man on YouTube who boasts that he can teach Hindi in three days. One day I might give him a try—but I've a feeling there's no shortcut.)

I was greeted with warmth and joy from my mother. She had been very accepting of my "other life," especially considering that she had no real knowledge of Australia—other than through cricket. There had been a one-day series going on between Australia, India, and Sri Lanka at the time of my first visit, and my mother said that after I'd left, whenever she saw cricket telecasts from Australia she would reach out to the screen, hoping I was in the crowd where her fingers were touching. Shekila and Kallu had traveled from their homes again to be there, too. I was welcomed back into the family without reserve.

My mother insisted that as her guests we all sat in her plastic chairs while she sat on the floor at my feet. We didn't need too many words to communicate how pleased we were to see each other, but it was terrific when Cheryl arrived to translate for us once more.

Still, talking was slow work. Often I would ask a one-sentence question, and then everyone else would talk among themselves in Hindi for what felt like five minutes before I got an answer back, usually just another single sentence. I guess Cheryl had to edit. She was very generous, a patient woman with a keen sense of humor, which was just as well, as my mother, Shekila, and Kallu all liked to joke around: it seems to be a family trait.

I also met a woman called Swarnima, who spoke perfect English and was so interested in my life story that she offered to come and translate for us for a while. I made arrangements to pay Swarnima for her time, but she returned the money. I learned from her parents that she'd been upset that I had seen it as a professional relationship and not an offer of friendship. In fact, I was merely overwhelmed by her generous spirit, and subsequently we became good friends.

Over several days, we all spent afternoons in my mother's front room, talking—and drinking chai and eating—usually in the company of relatives and friends, with Swarnima translating over the noise of the rusty little fan in the old bamboo rafters of the roof. My mother seemed to fear that I was still undernourished, even though twenty-five years of an Australian diet had certainly fixed that, and she kept trying to feed me. Being with her in the kitchen area made me recall when we were kids, huddled around the earth stove to watch her cooking. The taste of her goat curry is one of my strongest memories from my early years in Ganesh Talai. I have eaten goat curry in many places over the course of my life, from wayside cafes to upmarket restaurants, but I can honestly say I've never tasted any comparable with the one my mother cooks over her little stove in the back room of her home. There is something about the balance of spices and the consistency of the meat—if goat is not cooked correctly, the fibrous meat sticks between your teeth—that she has down to perfection. I know that sounds like a typical proud son's praise, but it's also the truth! I've cooked a lot of goat curries at home in Tasmania following the recipe I got from my mother on my first visit, but hers is always the best.

We talked a lot during this visit about how the family had never entirely written off the idea that I might come back. My mother had seen Guddu's body and therefore knew for sure he had died, but she admitted that they didn't mourn me as they did him because they couldn't quite believe I was dead. They had received some curious assurance in this belief. My mother never stopped praying for my return, and visited many priests and religious leaders in the community, asking for help and guidance. They always told her I was healthy and happy in good circumstances, and, amazingly, if asked where I was, they would point a finger to the south and say, "He's in that direction."

They did what they could to find me. It was an impossible task, of course—they had no idea where I could have gone. But my mother spent every spare bit of money looking for me—paying people to search, and even occasionally traveling around the area herself, from town to town, asking for any word. Kallu said they had talked a lot with police in Burhanpur and Khandwa—and that he had worked extra time to earn more money to help fund the family's searches. They never learned anything.

They couldn't have had "child missing" posters printed even

if they could have raised the money, because there weren't any photos of me. Praying was all they had left to do.

I began to realize that just as my search for my mother had in some ways shaped my life, her faith that I was alive had shaped hers. She couldn't search, but she did the next best thing: she stayed still. In conversation, I had wondered why she was still living in Ganesh Talai, when she could have gone to Burhanpur and lived with Kallu and his wife. She replied that she had wanted to stay near the house she had been living in when I disappeared, so that if I ever returned, I would be able to find her. I was bowled over by the thought. It's true that if she'd moved farther away, I would have had no chance of tracking her down. The strength of my mother's maternal instincts—her belief that I hadn't died and that I would someday return—seems to me now one of the most incredible aspects of this whole story.

I've experienced so many coincidences that I've just learned to accept them—even to be grateful for them. Kallu and Shekila told me they had always treasured their memories of us playing together and taking baths together as children—all the fun and mischief of our earliest years. Right from the start in Hobart, I used to imagine them in India each night before I went to sleep. I, like them, would think about the good times we had shared together, and tried to send my mother messages that I was all right and thinking of her and the family, hoping that they were still alive and well. Could a strong emotional bond create a kind of telepathic connection? It sounds far-fetched, but I've been through so much that defies reason that I can't entirely dismiss the idea. It seems to me that somehow the message was received.

Finally, my mother told me that one day she was praying to Allah for blessings on her family when an image of me appeared in her mind. The very next day, I walked back into Ganesh Talai and into her life.

During this visit, we also talked about how our lives were changing since my return. My mother told me that because of the publicity from the news reports, many families wished for their daughters to marry me, but she wanted me to know that any decision about marriage would be my decision and mine alone. I tried again to explain about Lisa, and that although we were very happy together, we didn't have any immediate plans to marry. She looked a little skeptical. My brother and sister were both married and had children; my mother said her only desire was that I did the same before she died, or, as she put it, before she "saw the road to God." She wanted me to have someone to take care of me in this world before she left it.

Both Kallu and Shekila said they would like to visit Australia at some point, although my mother felt too frail to make the journey. Shekila said she didn't need to see kangaroos or the Sydney Opera House, but she did want to see the house in which

I was raised. They wanted to meet my Australian family and told me they prayed for them every day at the mosque.

One of the most touching things my mother said to me was that if I ever wanted to come back to live in India, she would build me a home and go out and work hard so that I could be happy. Of course, my intention was the reverse: I wanted to give *her* a home and do everything I could to make her happy.

Money can be a tricky subject in families, but I wanted to share the good fortune I'd had. By the standards of my Indian family, I was a wealthy man, with an annual salary they could only dream about. But I was aware that I had to tread carefully, because I didn't want the issue of money to complicate or taint our new relationship.

The four of us discussed what arrangements would be of most benefit. My mother's new work as a housecleaner earned her about 1,200 rupees a month—a much greater sum than she earned when I was little but still a pittance, even in the context of regional India. We worked out a way for me to supplement her income. When I told my siblings I wanted to buy my mother a house, we discussed whether she might leave Ganesh Talai and live closer to Shekila or Kallu. But she was happy where she knew people well, and now that I'd returned, she decided that she wanted to stay in the neighborhood she had lived in all her life. So we resolved to find her something there, possibly even the place she was in now but with some much-needed repairs.

. . .

Inevitably, the subject of my father came up. My brother and sister were both completely unforgiving of him. They didn't doubt he would have seen the publicity surrounding my return but were adamant they'd turn him away if he appeared, however contrite he was. He had abandoned us when we were children and needed his help, and they felt he had to live with the decision he'd made. They also blamed him for the loss of Guddu—if he hadn't left us, Guddu wouldn't have been forced into his dangerous work on the railways. In their view, the lines of fate went back from Guddu's death and my disappearance to the day that my father brought his new woman into our home and presented her to our then-pregnant mother.

But although my family had sworn they would never have anything to do with him again, no matter what the circumstances, I couldn't find it in myself to feel the same. If my father genuinely regretted his behavior, then I could forgive him. Perhaps because I'd also made a decision that spiraled out of my control, I could imagine that he might have made a bad decision, and everything else had rolled forward from there. I couldn't hate him for making mistakes. He remained my father—even if I didn't really know him—and couldn't help but feel that my reunion with my past was incomplete without his role in it.

I had always had doubts he would be interested in seeing me, but toward the end of my stay, I received word from someone who was still in touch with him. He had indeed heard the reports of my return and had been angry that no one in the family had contacted him. He had recently been unwell and wanted to see me. The message captured my dilemma almost perfectly—despite the unsympathetic tone, I couldn't entirely harden my heart against him in his illness. However, there wasn't time to go to Bhopal, let alone raise the question with the family and seek their blessing. It was something I would have to let go for the time being.

Someone I had been eager to meet for a long time was Rochak, a local lawyer in his twenties who was the administrator of the Facebook group "Khandwa: My Home Town." He visited me at the hotel and it was nice to finally put a face to the name. His Facebook group had been crucial in confirming that I had found the right place. Rochak had also helped me work out the best way to travel to Khandwa from where I sat at my computer in Hobart. Facebook had helped lead me back to my family as much as Google Earth had.

I was pleased to be able to thank Rochak in person. He was genuinely delighted at the role he and his Facebook friends had played in my story, confirming details like the location of the fountain and cinema near Khandwa Station (once he had realized the cinema I was referring to had closed down). Unfortunately, he forgot at the time to send me some photos to confirm it, and I hadn't pressed him. Now Rochak said he realized he could have been more helpful had he known why I was asking, but I'd been nervous and coy about telling anyone what I was up to.

Rochak was out of town when the story of my homecoming broke, but he quickly worked out what had happened when he came back to find that his Khandwa Facebook group suddenly had 150 new members, half of whom not only didn't live in Khandwa but weren't even Indians.

He liked the way the Internet was putting people in far-flung regional places like Khandwa in touch with others around the world, as it was expanding people's horizons and helping them build relationships that once would have been impossible. Some people deride Facebook relationships and say you should get real friends in the real world. Rochak helped me online in the most profound way—surely there is no better basis for friendship.

Before he left, Rochak reminded me of the Hindu saying "Everything is written": destiny takes its inevitable path.

He thought my finding my home and family was a fulfillment of destiny, as was his helping me. Rochak had also helped me in one final way, by organizing a car and driver to take me on the hour-and-a-half trip to Burhanpur, where I was to stay the night before embarking on a journey with painful memories.

I had a train to catch.

13.

_____

Returning

There was one more thing I felt I had to do before I could put to rest some of the ghosts of my past. I wanted to go back to Kolkata as an adult, and to get there I would take a train from Burhanpur, just as I'd done as an imprisoned, panicked five-year-old, and see what memories it brought back.

In India, there is no such thing as simply making a rail booking. With the immense pressure of limited seats, a booking has to be certified beyond any possible challenge to ensure that when you get on the train, there is no one already sitting in your seat and that it is yours for the entire journey. This is made all the more difficult when you don't really know where you're going—even as an adult, I needed some help to work out what train it might have been that took me across the country.

I had first met Swarnima at the Khandwa station, having just abandoned a long queue at the ticket window when I realized that being unable to speak Hindi was going to make this trip even more difficult than it already promised to be. I had been feeling a bit defeated by the whole process, so her help was invaluable. Trains only go northeast or southwest out of Burhanpur, and together we worked out that both directions provided a possible route to Kolkata—one involved going south to Bhusawal, a more significant rail hub, from which there was a line heading roughly east across the country, and the other meant heading northeast before eventually arcing southeast toward the West Bengal capital. The northerly journey could be made without changing trains.

When I was being shown the two routes I might have taken twenty-five years earlier, I had to face up to the uncertainty of my memories of that time. Clearly, I had been wrong about one important detail. I had always thought I had woken up on the train and arrived in Kolkata later the same day, having traveled roughly twelve to fifteen hours. That was what I'd always told everyone, and indeed, it was the basis for a lot of my searching on Google. But there was simply no way to get from Burhanpur to Kolkata in that time. It's a 1,680-kilometer rail journey on the northerly route, and only a hundred kilometers less to go east via Bhusawal. The trip can take up to twenty-nine hours. I knew I got on the train in Burhanpur during the night, so I must have spent an additional night in transit. Maybe I slept through the entire second night. Or perhaps, as a terrified five-year-old, waking and sleeping between fits of panic and crying, I just lost track of time altogether. Either way, it was clearly a longer journey than I had remembered.

This explained why my meticulous searching of Google Earth was fruitless for so long. Not only did I spend a long time looking in the wrong areas of the country, but even when I was looking west, the rough boundary I had calculated based on how far I might have gone in my imagined time frame was much too close to Kolkata. I only found Burhanpur in the end by taking an incredibly fortuitous look outside my search boundary. Might I have found it more quickly if I'd got the time right? Perhaps, but perhaps not—as I'd decided that the only reliable method was to follow train lines out from Kolkata, I still would have spent a long time examining them, and I would have had to trace them further. I suppose once I'd exhausted my search zone, I would have widened it and kept going.

As I wondered which of the two routes I should book a seat on, another long-held assumption was challenged. I had always been certain that after Guddu and I had jumped off our train, I had slept on a bench, woken up to find a train in front of me, and boarded it, all without moving from the platform. As we'd traveled south from Khandwa to Burhanpur, any train on the same line would almost certainly have also been heading south, and you can't get to Kolkata that way without changing trains. I had to concede that either I was wrong about not moving from the platform where Guddu left me—in which case I might well have boarded a northbound train and been spirited directly to Kolkata—or I went south and at some point indeed changed trains.

As I've mentioned, my memories of that frightful night are not entirely clear, and sometimes I feel there are things I've only dimly remembered. Occasionally, I get flashes of them—so although my most prominent memory is that once I was on the train I was unable to escape it, I do have a disjointed, fragmentary image of the train at a station and my getting off it and jumping on another train. This is a flicker in the back of my mind, quite separate from my memories of the train ride, and I'm uncertain of it. But could it mean I initially made the trip south and then—because the train ended its service or I realized I was heading the wrong way—I switched trains to try to get back? It was possible, and that meant I might have reached Bhusawal and accidentally boarded an eastbound service to Kolkata.

Once the chance of my having changed trains was factored in, there was no way of determining which of the two routes I was most likely to have taken. A switch at Bhusawal might have sent me snaking east, but I might also have successfully switched to a train heading back north toward Burhanpur, then slept through the stop and been dragged off on the northeast route to

Kolkata. Perhaps the southbound train I originally boarded turned back north at some point while I slept, or maybe the carriage I was on was transferred to another engine, which did the same. I had to concede I was unlikely to ever work this particular equation out—it would remain a mystery.

I felt that if I couldn't know for certain that I was retracing my trip exactly, then which route I chose maybe didn't really matter—the point was to travel the distance and get a sense of the immensity of the journey, and perhaps to shake loose some more buried memories or put some lingering ones to rest. I wanted to recall more of the details of my trip to figure out how I'd arrived in Calcutta, yet not stir up some of the terrifying things that happened to me when I was lost. With that in mind, I thought I'd stick with my main memory of being trapped aboard for the duration and take the most direct, northeasterly path. To be completely honest, I chose this also partly because it was the easiest to organize and the most comfortable—there was a service that left Burhanpur at dawn, whereas the southerly route required further travel to Bhusawal late at night and waiting until the wee hours for a train headed east.

The train I decided I would take, then, was the Kolkata Mail, which had plied the same route in the eighties, when it was known as the Calcutta Mail. It started in Mumbai, on India's west coast, and reached Burhanpur at 5:20 a.m.—which is why I needed to be there overnight—before making its way to its namesake eastern capital. In fact, this particular service wasn't very likely to be the one I boarded as a child, even if I did somehow end up on the northeasterly route. It was scheduled to stop at Burhanpur Station for just two minutes, during which time a conductor would check off the names of the new passengers.

How could I have jumped on and fallen asleep before it left the station? And I know there was no conductor around back then; indeed, it's a mystery how I didn't see one during my entire ordeal. Conductors are a regular presence on interstate trains, which is one of the reasons I couldn't get far out of Kolkata when I was trying to find my way back: because I was avoiding conductors, I was probably unwittingly boarding only local trains. (There was an element of luck in this: if I had succeeded in leaving Kolkata, the chances were strong that rather than being taken to Madhya Pradesh, I would have ended up somewhere else again, amplifying the problem. I could have been doubly, then trebly lost. Outside Kolkata, I was unlikely to have been taken to an adoption agency.)

I didn't want thoughts about retracing my steps exactly to complicate things further. So having chosen the Kolkata Mail with the help of Rochak and Swarnima, everything was put in place. When the car to Burhanpur arrived, I set off for a final visit to my mother. By this time, Swarnima had returned to work in Pune, where she lived, but fortunately Cheryl was able to help with our last few minutes of conversation over a parting cup of chai. We posed for family photographs together; looking at those photos now, I find it striking how much I resemble my mother and siblings.

My mother and Cheryl accompanied me out to the car, and we passed a crowd of curious locals who'd gathered to watch the lost boy take his leave from his family again. This was an especially wrenching departure—we were reenacting the day I got lost. The last time I'd left on this particular journey, as a child, I hadn't said good-bye; now a quarter of a century later, my mother hugged me tightly, smiling all the while. Although it must have been as emotional for her as it was for me—even more so—this time she wasn't worried that I wouldn't come back. She knew for absolute certain now that we would always find each other.

I spent the evening in the courtyard restaurant of my hotel in Burhanpur, watching the last skyrockets of people's Diwali festival stockpiles light up the sky. I knew taking the Kolkata Mail wouldn't solve all the mysteries of my original journey. In fact, I was nervous at the prospect of the trip and about which other memories—recollections that have been the cornerstone of my identity—it might challenge.

I'd been told it was a good idea to get to Burhanpur Station an hour early to be on the safe side, so when I eventually turned in, I set my alarm for ten past three in the morning. I needn't have bothered—a knock on my door woke me, and I opened it to a young man in a military jacket, his face almost entirely obscured by a head scarf, who identified himself as an auto-rickshaw driver booked for me by the hotel desk. The hotel had no hot water, so I woke myself up with a jet of cold water and at four o'clock checked out and stepped into the darkness outside. We loaded my luggage into the three-wheeler auto and zoomed off down silent streets, past new blocks of flats, fully built, half built, and according to the many colorful billboards, coming soon. I saw these signs all over India, each one boasting a new building with a gym, pool, and all the mod conveniences, which reflected the economic boom.

It was cool before the sun rose. I had barely slept from the anticipation of my journey, so the cooler air was a welcome help in keeping me awake. Around us, I saw silhouettes of cows sleeping under awnings and pigs huddled together.

We pulled up outside the station, where a few people sat around in groups and others slept on the ground, blankets pulled up to cover them entirely, which made them look unsettlingly like they were in body bags. Inside, a brightly lit red sign told me the train was an hour late. So much for careful planning.

I had ample time to look around the station from which my first journey to Kolkata had begun. Even though it seemed much the same as I remembered it, some things had changed. I recalled the platform benches were made with wooden slats, including the one I slept on that first night. Now the seats were of polished granite within a wooden frame. Also, while Ganesh Talai seemed much filthier now than when I was little, back then the Burhanpur station had been dirty and full of litter but now was very clean. On the wall there was a poster of a police officer nabbing a man spitting on the platform.

Looking across to the opposite platform, I felt sure it was the one that I'd boarded from, trying to find Guddu. I simply must have traveled south initially, even if I somehow came back through Burhanpur for the northern route. My head swam with all the possible permutations.

A chai man plying his trade on the other platform noticed me looking over and caught my attention. With little else to do, I waved to him that, yes, I'd welcome a cup. He gestured at me to stay where I was, then jumped down and crossed the tracks, balancing my cup on his metal tray. Just as he'd clambered back onto his platform, a freight train came thundering through the station—an awesome, frightening spectacle. In Australia, trains tend to slow down at stations, but here massive trains hurtled through at regular intervals, shaking the platform. The chai man lived with these trains and judged his timing expertly, but how much harder it would be to make those judgments if you were distracted by grief or guilt.

I couldn't help imagining what would happen if you made a mistake. Was that what had happened to Guddu?

Despite the confusion about which platform I'd boarded from and whether I'd stayed aboard a single train, I still have clear, if disjointed, images in my head of the train journey itself. Clambering aboard and looking for Guddu, then curling up on one of the seats and going back to sleep. Wakening to bright daylight in an empty carriage, hurtling along. I have some memory of the train stopping at least at one point along its route, with no one around, and of always being unable to open any of the doors to the outside. I was confused and frightened, and I suppose it's not surprising I didn't keep good track of time. It must have felt an eternity to a child of that age.

By small degrees daylight came, and people were still arriving at the platform in dribs and drabs—apparently the train's late arrival was predictable. Some were wrapped up as if the temperature was below freezing—in such a hot place, the dawn cool could be uncomfortable for the locals. They hefted all manner of suitcases, bags and bundles, and domestic appliances taped up tightly in cardboard cartons. As the light strengthened I saw the big water tower behind the station, which had helped me identify Burhanpur from the sky. I was lucky it hadn't been knocked down or moved, or I wouldn't have recognized the place.

The Kolkata Mail slipped into the station as dawn arrived. It had already traveled five hundred kilometers in eight hours northeast from Mumbai, on the Arabian Sea. I stood at the point at which my assigned carriage was to draw up and, sure enough, a conductor consulted his list before ushering me onto the carriage, where I found my allocated seat. I didn't plan on doing things quite as hard as I had the first time around—I'd booked a first-class compartment, which I'll admit I hoped would be like the Orient Express as per Agatha Christie, but it fell a little short. There were no luxury carriages on this train, or staff in starched white uniforms with gold buttons offering gin and tonics on silver trays. The configuration of the carriages was very similar to the low-class one I'd boarded as a child: sets of single seats facing each other at the window, and across the aisle a sort of open compartment of facing bench seats, which could be used for sleeping. The appointments in this class were better, of course, but the worn maroon leather seats were still quite hard. Fortunately, I wouldn't have to sit for the whole journey. My ticket also bought me one of the bench bunks across the aisle, and at least for the time being, I had the area to myself.

It's another mystery that my recollection of my first journey is of my carriage being empty from the first time I woke until its arrival in Kolkata. An empty train carriage in India is unheard of, yet I am certain that mine was. Surely if someone boarded, even a conductor, I would have asked for help. There may have been people traveling in the adjacent carriages, of course, and I wouldn't have known—I didn't see or hear anyone else. I had remained sitting in my empty carriage, waiting for someone to open a door. Was the carriage locked up and being hauled off for repair? Did I somehow end up on a work train, not meant for passengers and not a scheduled service at all? If so, why would it have gone all the way to Kolkata?

As the train started to inch away from the platform, I shivered, remembering how this moment had begun the process of my getting hopelessly lost. But I was here to set something right by confronting the fear I'd had and the circumstances back then, and by traveling the distance again as a more comprehending, capable adult. I was also returning to Kolkata to see again the places where I'd survived on the streets, and to visit Mrs. Sood and the others at Nava Jeevan, the place where my fortunes had taken a dramatic turn. As the train picked up speed and cleared the Burhanpur platform, I looked around the carriage and wondered what personal journeys my fellow passengers were making.

When I was a child, air travel in India was reserved for only the most important people: politicians, business moguls and their families, or Bollywood film stars. The railways were the veins of the country—circulating goods, people, and money. Trains brought glimpses of the more affluent city life to our backwater town in the middle of rural India. It's not surprising that we spent a lot of time hanging around railway stations watching people come and go, making whatever money we could by selling things to passengers—as Guddu did with the tooth-brush and toothpaste packs that got him arrested—or begging for whatever they might give us. The railways were our only connection with the rest of the country—the rest of the world as we knew it—and for most people that's probably still the case.

The trains aren't terribly fast, though. When Swarnima and I booked the Kolkata Mail, I learned that it averaged fifty to sixty kilometers an hour. My Indian college friends had overestimated typical train speeds somewhat, which was lucky, as it made my original search field larger than it ought to have been, based on my faulty recollection of a half-day trip. Had they known how slow the trains were, it might have taken me longer to get around to searching farther afield. I settled back in my seat, with nearly thirty hours of travel ahead of me.

At first most of my fellow passengers kept to their cabin bunks, catching up on sleep. But eventually people could be heard moving around and murmuring, before curtains were drawn back to reveal traveling families waking up and facing the day.

We had traveled for just over an hour when I experienced a poignant moment. If it was this northeastern route I had been on as a child, I would have passed through my hometown, Khandwa. I knew we were headed there, of course, but rolling into town just as it was coming to life for the day's activity inev-itably made me wonder if I'd been on this train as a sleeping five-year-old. Had I awakened there, I might well have had the opportunity to get off the train and simply go home, presuming Guddu had met some friends or found something he needed to do. I could have climbed into my own bed, disappointed I hadn't got to stay away with my brother for longer. And then none of the things that followed—my experiences on the streets in Kolkata, my rescue, and my adoption—would have occurred. I would not be Australian. You would not be reading my story. Instead, I possibly slept through a two-minute stop at Khandwa, not far from where my mother and sister were probably asleep themselves, and was transported away from what would have been a very different life, the one I was born into.

As thoughts like these trailed through my mind, the day got under way and the sounds on the train became louder. Each voice had to be pitched to overcome the rumbling and clattering of the train on the tracks. Everybody seemed to have a mobile phone, all blaring with ringtones of popular songs from Hindi films, and there was constant conversation. In the background was what sounded like a compilation CD of many different styles of contemporary Hindi music, including jazz and even what seemed to be Hindi yodeling. Wallahs began their regular trips up and down the carriage, selling food and drink with a sort of chant: "Chai, chai, brek-fist, brek-fist, om-lit, om-lit."

Stretching my legs on a little walk, I found the pantry car, where cooks stripped to the waist fried huge quantities of chickpea and lentil snacks in boiling oil, as well as mountains of sliced potato in vast vats. The vats and pots rested on bricks and were heated by enormous jets of gas, and the cooks tended them with long wooden paddles—it was amazing to watch them do all this on a bumpy train.

There weren't any carriages on the Kolkata Mail like the one I'd been trapped in, with barred windows and the rows of hard wooden benches. You also couldn't walk between the carriages on that train—the doors only opened onto the platform. It seemed more and more likely that on my first trip, I'd been in some sort of carriage that wasn't in use—the bustle and noise of an Indian train are inescapable, and the chance that the carriage would otherwise have remained empty was nil.

As we traveled northeast, the landscape out the window was as I remembered it—flat, dusty, and seemingly endless—although this time I was composed enough to see some of the texture and details of the place: expanses of cotton and wheat fields, irrigated crops and chili plants with so many chilis on them they looked red from a distance, as well as the usual cows, goats, donkeys, horses, pigs, and dogs. Combine harvesters worked side by side with bullocks and carts, and farmers harvested by hand, building piles of hay. There were villages of tiny brick-and-plaster houses painted in pastel colors like pale pink, lime green, and faded sky blue, with old roofs of terra-cotta tiles that looked like they could fall off at any moment. We also passed through tiny railway stations painted in the brick red, yellow, and white patterns of Indian Railways. I must have seen a few of these when I hurtled along those decades ago; I must have been begging for the train to stop at one. I wondered whether anyone in these fields looked up at a passing train and saw a small face at the window looking out with fright.

I thought about Kolkata, and found that I was more anxious than nervous. Even though parts of it would be full of memories, it would also be like visiting a place for the first time. I was lost in Calcutta, but I was returning to Kolkata. Both of us had changed, and I was looking forward to seeing how much.

Night had begun to descend as I had these thoughts, and by the time I'd folded the seat down and unpacked the Indian Railways linen from its paper covering, it was dark. I lay down on my bunk and found I could still see out the window to watch the lit-up temples, bicycle lights, and house lights flash by as the train rolled on.

With the train's bumping and swaying, an unexpected sense of well-being came over me. I felt at ease lying there, bouncing along in my bunk amid the chatter of people speaking in languages that sounded familiar but which I didn't understand. During the day, I'd had a chat with a curious little boy from the next open compartment. He was about ten years old and keen to try out his school English with "What's your name?" and "Where are you from?" He seemed to be able to tell that I was not from

India despite my looks—maybe it was my clothes, or that I didn't join in conversations in Hindi or Bengali. When I told him I was from Australia, he mentioned Shane Warne. After talking about cricket for a bit, he asked me, "Are you married?" When I said I wasn't, he told me how disappointed he was for me. "Who are your family?" he asked next, and I found myself hesitating. "My family lives in Tasmania, but I also have family here, in Khandwa, in Madhya Pradesh," I said at last. That seemed to satisfy him, and I realized that it had also begun to satisfy me.

Late in the morning of the next day, we began the approach to Kolkata. From the vantage point of the train, I could watch how the tracks we were on merged with many others, so there came to be numerous sets of rails in parallel running into Howrah Station. I might have traveled these lines as a boy, but who knows? I might not have managed to get on any that came out to this western edge of the city. There seemed to be an impossible number of lines, which could take a person in every possible direction. I was seeing the evidence that I'd never stood a chance of finding my way back.

The train seemed to speed up now, passing through level crossings where trucks and cars and auto-rickshaws waited, with everyone blasting their horns. It wasn't long before we were deep in one of the world's biggest cities, along with somewhere between fifteen and twenty million other people. It was 12:20 p.m., exactly thirty hours after my departure from Burhanpur, when the train coasted into the massive, red-brick Howrah Railway Station, which gave me tingles of recognition as we inched up to the platform and stopped.

I had returned.

When I got off the train, I took a minute or two to simply stand in the middle of the busy station concourse and let the crowd rush by me, just as I did back then. This time people surged around me, as they would any adult standing in their way, whereas the last time I had stood here, pleading for help, I don't think they even saw me. On one hand, I believed that among all those people there wasn't one willing to take the time to help a lost child. On the other, I wondered whether any other reaction was possible—in a crowd this size, everyone was anonymous, invisible. Why would one upset kid be of any particular interest amid all the activity of the place? And if anyone stopped, how much patience would they have had for being mumbled at in Hindi about a place they'd never heard of?

The station building itself was hauntingly familiar. I'd begged in it, slept in and around it, and spent those weeks making futile train trips to try to get out of it. It had been my home at a most traumatic time of my life. But now it was just a train station, albeit a very big one, and busier than any I'd ever seen. There wasn't much to gain from hanging around when I didn't have to.

I didn't notice any homeless children inside—perhaps they

were more likely to be moved these days—but I did see a couple of small groups once I walked outside the building into the brutally strong sun. They had that unmistakable look about them: grubby from street living and somehow simultaneously idle and alive to opportunities, such as begging or stealing from someone passing close by. Could I have ever found myself part of a gang, or had I been too wary or naïve?

It's hard to imagine I could have survived the streets on my own for much longer than I did. I would have become one of these kids, or dead.

I found a taxi. Before long, I was heading to the hotel my travel agent had booked, which turned out to be quite upmarket, with Indian and Western food, bars, a gym, and an infinity pool. I went for a swim: at the pool you could lounge around on recliner chairs on the pool deck or swim over to the infinity edge and look out at Kolkata, many floors down and extending as far as the eye could see, with its smog, traffic, chaos, and poverty.

One of the main reasons I'd come to Kolkata was to meet someone who'd played an absolutely central part in my life. Once I had learned that Mrs. Saroj Sood was not only still alive but still working for ISSA, I'd made arrangements to visit her in her office. I linked up with my Bengali translator and took a taxi through the mad traffic, dust, and stink of untreated sewage.

The ISSA office was in a run-down Victorian building in Kolkata's Park Street quarter, an area with many restaurants and bars and the Flurys tearoom, which people visit for the famous cucumber sandwiches and cake. Amid all this high life and refinement, it's a center of salvation.

I passed through an outer office, where staff at desks worked through large stacks of papers. Then I saw her, scrutinizing a computer monitor and surrounded by official-looking files in the cramped inner office, an old air conditioner stuck hazardously onto the wall above her—Mrs. Sood. The place looked exactly as it had twenty-five years before.

Mrs. Sood's eyes widened when I walked in and introduced myself. We shook hands and then embraced. She was now in her eighties, but she said she remembered me well from when I was a child, despite the number of children who had passed through her care since then. "I remember your mischievous grin. Your face has not changed," she told me in her excellent English, smiling widely. We had last seen each other in Hobart a few years after my adoption, when she had arrived to escort another adoptee.

She asked me about both of my mothers and then asked a social worker she worked with, Soumeta Medhora, to find my adoption file. While they talked about where it might be, I looked at the pin-up boards on the walls covered with pictures of smiling children.

Mrs. Sood had been working to help children in need in this same office for thirty-seven years. In that time, she had arranged adoptions for around two thousand Indian children, some to families in India and others to families overseas. She had a daughter of her own, a successful businesswoman who told people that she had "donated her mother" to the work of adoption.

Born in Delhi, Mrs. Sood gained a law degree and became interested in adoption. She arranged her first adoption within India in 1963, and three years later succeeded in assisting a Swedish exchange student, Madeleine Kats, to adopt an Indian girl in Sweden. Kats became a journalist, and when she wrote of her experience and mentioned Mrs. Sood, other people from abroad started asking for her help to arrange adoptions. And so it all began.

Mrs. Sood moved to Calcutta, receiving training from the Missionaries of Charity, the order that Mother Teresa founded; indeed, she was blessed by Mother Teresa herself. She gained some other influential patrons—the president of the All India Women's Conference, and a renowned independence freedom fighter, Ashoka Gupta—and with their support registered ISSA in 1975. Seven years later, the organization set up the orphanage I stayed in, Nava Jeevan, meaning "new life."

Mrs. Sood told me that my adoption had gone through easily, especially compared to the average international adoption today. She said that intercountry adoption was now managed by a central authority rather than directly through agencies like ISSA, but that measures designed to "streamline" procedures had instead made the process ever more complicated and lengthy.

It now commonly took a year, and sometimes as long as five years, for all the paperwork, arrangements, and procedures to be finalized. I could feel her frustration, and I knew that Mum felt the same way—she had become a passionate advocate for making international adoption easier after going through the delays in adopting Mantosh and seeing how the extra time in adverse circumstances had affected him.

In 1987, when Mum and Dad had received approval for adoption, they met with an ISSA staff member escorting adoptees to Australia, who showed them my file. They immediately agreed they would take me. Two weeks later Mrs. Sood visited them herself, on a trip to escort my fellow Nava Jeevan adoptees Abdul and Musa, and brought back the photo book my new parents had prepared for me.

I asked Mrs. Sood whether it was unusual for families abroad who adopted an Indian child to adopt a second, even if they were not related. She said it was quite common—the first child would get lonely, or culturally isolated, or the parents just enjoyed the experience so much, they wanted to repeat it.

Tea was brought, and while we drank it together, Mrs. Medhora returned with my file and I was able to see the agency's actual documents of my adoption. The pages were a little faded and fragile, almost as if they could fall apart at a touch. Attached to the file was a photograph of me in Australia, which my parents had sent after I arrived. I was grinning and holding a golf club, standing in front of an old-fashioned golf buggy. There was also a photocopy of my passport, with its photograph of the six-year-old me looking steadily into the camera. My official documents and passport all had my name as "Saru," which is how it had been recorded since I arrived in the police station. It was Mum and Dad who had decided "Saroo" was a more Anglicized spelling, more like it sounded.

The file revealed that I had come to the attention of the authorities in Calcutta after I was accepted into the custody of officers at Ultadanga Police Station on April 21, 1987. I was assessed and taken to Liluah, the juvenile home, where I was classified as a child in need of care. There were two other categories for children at Liluah—those whose parents had come to the attention of the police and courts, and those who themselves had committed offenses—and we were all bunked in together.

The picture of what happened to me then became a little clearer. I had been in Liluah for one month and then handed over to the care of ISSA at a hearing in the Juvenile Court on May 22. Mrs. Sood would regularly visit Liluah to ask about new admissions needing care and, where appropriate, she would apply to the court to have them handed over temporarily to ISSA. Her agency was given two months to find the child's family and reunite them or have an orphaned child declared "free" to be adopted into a new family. If these efforts were unsuccessful, the child would have to return and remain in Liluah, although ISSA could continue to pursue their case. This was Mantosh's fate, as it took ISSA two years to untangle the difficulties within his family and have him released for adoption.

In my case, staff at ISSA took a photo of me—the first I'd ever had taken—and it was published on June 11 in a Bengali daily newspaper with a notification that I was a lost child. On June 19 they published it in the *Oriya Daily,* a widely read newspaper published in the state of Orissa (now known as Odisha), because they thought I might have boarded the train in the coastal city of Brahmapur. Of course, there was no response—it was miles away from where I actually lived. I was therefore officially declared a "neglected child" and was formally made "free" for adoption, after my agreement, on June 26.

My case for adoption by the Brierleys came up for hearing on August 24 and was approved—so I was in Nava Jeevan for two months. I was issued a passport on September 14, departed India on September 24, and arrived in Melbourne the following day, September 25, 1987. From the moment the teenager with the handcart had taken me into the police station until the moment I stepped off the aircraft in Melbourne, the entire process had taken only a little over five months. Mrs. Sood said that if I was being adopted now, the process would take years. Mrs. Medhora corrected a misconception I'd had about how I had come to be chosen for release from Liluah, which I thought was because I had been in good health. The real reason was because I'd been lost—

ISSA's first intention had been to reunite me with my parents. Children with disabilities of all kinds were released from Liluah if it was thought there was a possibility they could be reunited with their families. Soon after my adoption went through, ISSA had managed to reunite two other lost children with their families after placing ads in the newspapers. But I'd simply had too little information for them to start a meaningful search.

In fact, they didn't even know that I'd spent some weeks on the streets of Kolkata. Confused and no doubt a little frightened about what was happening to me, I'd just answered the questions that were put to me. And even if they'd asked me directly about it, I probably wouldn't have been able to tell them much— I was poor and uneducated, and my language was too limited to be able to communicate much. ISSA had only learned that I'd been on the streets years later, when Mum told them after she'd learned about it from me. Mrs. Sood said they had been astounded. Most couldn't imagine a five-year-old from a small town surviving on the streets of Kolkata alone for a few days, let alone several weeks. I had been incredibly lucky.

After Mrs. Sood and I had said our fond good-byes, and I'd thanked her again for everything she'd done for me, a driver took Mrs. Medhora, my interpreter, and me down yet more congested roads, past a new metro train line under construction, to a quiet residential street of apartment blocks in the northern suburbs, looking for Nava Jeevan. In fact, the orphanage had moved to a new location, and the building I knew as Nava Jeevan was now used as a free day-care center for children of poor working mothers.

At first I was convinced we'd come to the wrong place. Mrs. Medhora tried to reassure me, but I was so certain of my memories that I thought she must have become confused with all the moving the orphanage had done over the years. It turned out that I didn't recognize the second story of the building because I'd never been in it—only babies lived upstairs.

When I went into the downstairs quarters, I found the Nava Jeevan I remembered. There were a dozen or so young children taking their afternoon nap stretched out on mats on the floor. These kids, though, were collected by their mothers and taken home at the end of the day.

Two more places to visit remained. First, we went to the Juvenile Court in which I was pronounced an orphan, in a suburban satellite town oddly named Salt Lake City, about half an hour's drive from central Kolkata. It was a dingy, nondescript building, and I didn't stay there long, on either visit. The second, though, was the Liluah home. Given my less than happy experiences there, it had promised to be a difficult visit, which I think was why I'd left it till last. I hadn't exactly been looking forward to seeing it again, though I knew my visit to the Kolkata of my childhood wouldn't be complete without it.

Once again ISSA kindly provided a car and driver, and we crossed the landmark Howrah Bridge and went past Howrah

Station, threading our way through narrow alleyways to reach the imposing building—almost a fortress. As the car pulled up outside, I saw again the massive red rusted gates that I have never been able to forget, with the small hatchway entrance to one side, just like a prison. The gate was immense in my childhood memory, and was still imposing now. The high brick walls were topped with metal spikes and jagged glass.

By now, as the blue sign over the entrance informed me, it had become a "Home for Girls and Women." Boys were sent elsewhere. Although it looked the same, and there were still guards on duty outside, it felt a little less brutal somehow—perhaps it was just that this time I was here as a visitor.

Mrs. Medhora had arranged for us to be admitted, so we went straight through a little doorway. Inside we came across a large pond that I barely remembered being there. The buildings appeared smaller and much less menacing than they had. But something about the atmosphere still made it feel like a place you would want to get out of as soon as possible.

We made a tour and I saw the same kinds of bunk-lined halls in which I had slept and dreamed of release. I would never have imagined when I left here that I would one day willingly return, yet here I was now, looking over the place, a tourist to my old terrors. But more than any other visit I made, Liluah put the pain of that past to rest at last. As I stood there, I thought about the time outsiders had breached what looked like a fortress, and wondered how that could have happened without someone turning a blind eye. No doubt there needed to be stricter controls in place to avoid such blights on the system. I felt more than thankful that I had survived my stay here and got out relatively unscathed. And I was glad to realize that it would be close to impossible for an outsider to sneak in now.

There was one last visit I had to make—not a particular building but an area. On my final day in Kolkata I returned to the streets near Howrah Station and the little group of cheap cafes and shops that still clung to the top of the banks of the Hooghly River. It remained a place for the less well-off, workers on a pittance, homeless people. There was still no sanitation, and a lot of people lived in makeshift lean-tos and stalls in the area. I walked around the shop stalls, recalling how I used to smell the mouthwatering fruits and fried foods on sale here, and marveled that I had been able to detect them at all over the stench of human waste mingled with diesel and petrol fumes and smoke from cooking fires.

I walked down to look at the river's edge, but the area between the shops and the water seemed to have been divided up into private housing plots. Just as I was trying to work out a way through, several mangy-looking dogs came my way up a little alley, nosing past my legs, and I decided I didn't want to put my anti-rabies shot to the test. I don't mind dogs on leashes, but to let these strays get close seemed risky. Instead, I took the footpath away from the row of shops to the impressive steel span of the Howrah Bridge, and before long joined the stream of people at the start of its pedestrian walkway, which links the city of Howrah with central Kolkata. When I first crossed it, I was escaping my terrifying experience with the men from the railway shack. Now I knew the bridge was a major Kolkata landmark, probably the best known in the city. It was one of the last major British projects before India achieved independence in 1947.

The masses of humanity crossing it, and the stream of vehicles of all kinds, were incredible. People pushed behind me and rushed toward me. Bearers moved to and from the railway station like ants walking to and from their nests, with astonishingly bulky loads balanced perfectly on their heads. Beggars lined the railing along the walkway, raising their steel bowls and amputated limbs and adding their chants to the boisterous noise of the bridge. The scale of human presence and activity almost made the bridge a community in itself. But the crowds also started to make me feel insignificant, as though I didn't exist.

How small I must have felt when I crossed it as a little kid.

The traffic noise was tremendous and there were clouds of blue smoke rising, momentarily cloaking the scene. I'd read that living with the air pollution of Sydney or Melbourne can reduce your life span, so I could only wonder by how much your life would be shortened here, breathing in this kind of pollution day in and day out.

Around a third of the way across the bridge, I stopped at the railing and looked back at the riverbank, to a place below the station and the shops, the area where I had somehow survived as a boy. Now there was a ferry jetty in the place I had walked along, and underneath the bridge the bank had been concreted. I couldn't see if the sadhus could still sleep there. I hadn't seen many sadhus during my return visits to India, but I didn't know if theirs was a lifestyle in decline or if it was just coincidental. I made a mental note to research this later. Those men felt like guardians to me when I'd slept near them or their shrines.

I looked down at the stone steps—the ghats—that led into the powerful tidal waters of the Hooghly, at the place where I had almost drowned, twice, and I thought about the homeless man who had plucked me from the water both times. He would almost certainly be dead by now. But like the teenager who later took me to the police station, he had given me another chance to live. He hadn't profited from his act in any way—unless he was a believer in karma—and I had never thanked him. I was too embarrassed and frightened by the attention when he pulled me out the second time. So as I stood there at the railing looking down at my past, I thanked that man, and then I thanked him again as the sun began to set and my last day in Kolkata ended in a smoky pink-gray haze.

It was time to go home.

Epilogue

The moment when my two mothers met for the first time was an incredible milestone. When the idea of filming their introduction had been floated by *60 Minutes* in Australia, to be featured as the centerpiece of a story about my experiences, I found myself once again apprehensive. There always seemed to be another emotional journey ahead of me yet to be traveled. Would Mum feel somehow less bonded to me when she met the woman who had given birth to me? Would she worry that Kamla, my mother, might demand my return? Would Kamla find it impossible to connect with Mum, or feel awkward about being thrust together with her in front of the cameras? I knew Mum was nervous about that, as well as about what would, amazingly, be her first visit to India.

Of course, I had always wanted to bring my two families together, and they had all spoken of looking forward to such a meeting. Despite finding the prospect a little daunting, I was disappointed my dad wasn't able to join us this time. For now, it was to be my mothers laying eyes on each other for the first time.

When the moment arrived in Ganesh Talai, with the *60 Minutes* crew in tow, time seemed to stand still. All concerns washed away as I watched my mothers—who had given me not just one life but two—embracing with tears in their eyes. How many events since I was a little boy had lined up to lead to this day? It was staggering.

We communicated through a translator, but the joy and love we shared didn't need much translation.

Mum greatly admired the strength of Kamla in surviving the many struggles of her life. It gives me great pleasure to be able to help my mother in India, however I can, including taking care of her rent and buying food—whatever might make things more comfortable for her. Typically, she resists, insisting that all she cares about is having me back in her life. Despite her soft protests, now that I have secured the dual citizenship that permits me to buy property within India, I plan to buy her a better home in Ganesh Talai, near her friends. Patience is required when doing business in the poor village, and I'm waiting on the paper-work, but Kallu, Shekila, and I have found Kamla a place just around the corner from where she waited for me all this time. We look forward to helping her move into her own home—her first.

I am also devoting time to helping another incredibly impor-tant woman in my life, without whom it would be unlikely that I would be here to write my story: Saroj Sood. I am assisting with repairs to the Nava Jeevan orphanage for abandoned babies and lost children. Words can't properly express my gratitude to Mrs. Sood and her dedicated staff at ISSA. If I can help her with her mission to care for children who find themselves in situations similar to that which befell me, I will do everything I can.

My desires for myself are less clear. Even as I poured all my efforts into tracking down my hometown and family, I was never searching in the hope of somehow getting back to the life I had missed. It wasn't a matter of needing to right a wrong nor one of wanting to return to where I "belong." I spent almost all of my life in Australia, and I have family bonds here that cannot be challenged or broken.

I wanted to know where I came from—to be able to look at a map and point to the place where I was born—and to throw light on some of the circumstances of my past. Most of all, though I tried to keep my expectations in check as insurance against disappointment, I hoped to find my Indian family so they would know what had happened to me. My bonds with them can never be broken, and I am deeply grateful that I now have the opportunity to renew our connection.

But I am not conflicted about who I am or where to call home. I now have two families, not two identities. I am Saroo Brierley.

Nonetheless, revisiting India and seeing the lives of my siblings and my mother has been a culturally enriching experience as well as a personal one. I look at my brother and sister, particularly, and admire their traditional focus on family and relationships. It is difficult to put into words, but I feel that perhaps there is something in the West we have lost in our impersonal suburbs and emphasis on individualism. I am not a religious person, and that likely won't change in a major way, but I am keen to learn more about the customs and beliefs of my Indian family, and to see if they offer some guidance for me.

I am also delighted to have met my niece and nephews, and I look forward to being a part of their lives and to provide them with whatever opportunities I am able to.

Had I not become lost—not gone out that night with Guddu, or had somehow found my way home soon after—my life would have been hugely different, of course. Much suffering could have been avoided. My family would not have endured the heartbreak of a missing son on top of the tragic death of another, and I would not have known the pain of separation and the cold fear that struck me in the train or on the Kolkata streets.

But my experiences have undoubtedly shaped who I am today, providing me with an unshakable faith in the importance of family—however it is formed—and a belief in the goodness of people and the importance of grasping opportunities as they are presented. I wouldn't wish to erase any of that. It's true, too, that my Indian family has received opportunities they would not have had otherwise had none of this taken place. I feel strongly that there is an element of destiny in these events, intertwining my two families, with me as the linchpin.

I know my mum and dad wouldn't wish for their lives to have been different, either, without me and Mantosh. I am unspeakably grateful to them for the love—and the life—they have given me, and I have nothing but admiration for their commitment to helping others who are less fortunate. I am confident that my finding my Indian home will bring my Australian family closer together rather than making anyone question our connection.

When I told Mantosh that I had found my family, he was naturally very happy for me. Some news of his sadly fractured family has filtered through to us from ISSA, and Mantosh has found my success in reuniting with my Indian family inspiring. Despite the painful memories of his childhood, and his struggles growing up, he has renewed his interest in trying to reconnect with his Indian mother. We're not sure if it is possible, but I would like nothing more than to see my brother achieve some of the peace of mind granted to me.

I was also delighted to celebrate my good fortune with Asra. In the early years, with our families having become firm friends, we kept in touch by phone quite often, and occasionally visited each other's homes interstate. Although we lost touch a little as we got older, as people do, we still catch up every now and then, with news of jobs, relationships, and life in general. There are some aspects of my experiences that only Asra and I can share, and I consider myself lucky to have such a friend.

When I look back at the process of my rediscovering Khandwa—the Google Earth searches that consumed me, in particular—I realize that I could have approached things differently, and might possibly have found what I was looking for more quickly. I could have been more forensic about the various "Burhanpur"-type towns and cities that appeared on maps, and could have considered those farther across the country from Kolkata. It's possible that deeper Internet searches might have ruled out some of these places straightaway, or at least narrowed the field. I might also have restricted my searches to train lines near a short list of "B" towns rather than pedantically tracing all routes out from Howrah Station to a roughly calculated perimeter, even if there was a juggernaut logic to my methods. Perhaps that would have delivered Khandwa more quickly, perhaps not. We all know what they say about hindsight.

But I went about my search the best way I could at the time. I don't have any regrets about how things transpired, with the exception of my brother's tragic death. I am astonished at the miraculous turns in my story—my mum's vision that led her to intercountry adoption, my Indian mother praying and seeing an image of me the day before we were reunited. Even the remarkable coincidence of finding myself at school in a place called Howrah. It is sometimes difficult not to imagine some forces at work that are beyond my understanding. While I don't have any urge to convert that into religious belief, I feel strongly that from my being a little lost boy with no family to becoming a man with two, everything was meant to happen just the way it happened. And I am profoundly humbled by that thought.

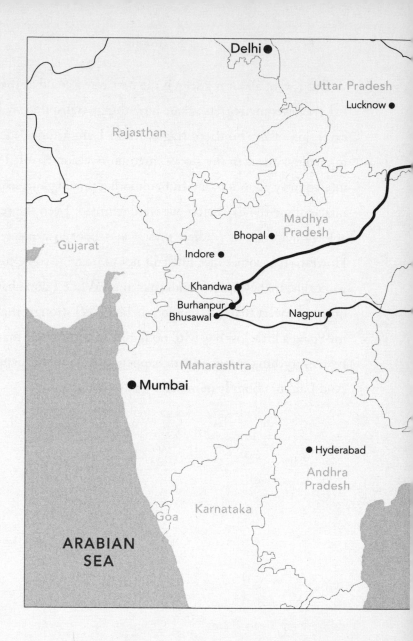

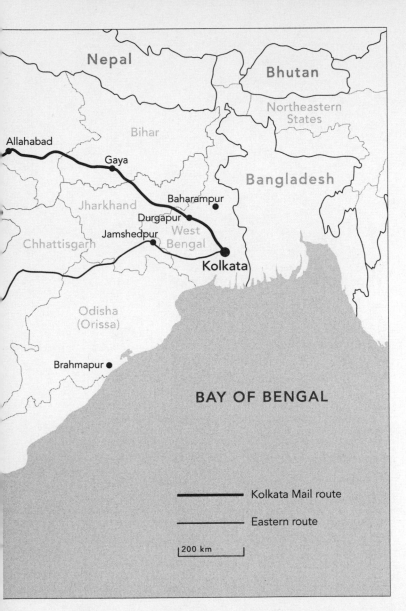

My Journey Across India

The two most likely rail routes from Burhanpur to Kolkata (assuming only one train change, or perhaps none), although I will never know for certain which was the one I took as a child. No one suspected I had been transported so far, which cruelly hindered all efforts to find my home and family. In 2012, I rode the Kolkata Mail, crossing the country in much greater comfort.

Acknowledgments

I offer my deep gratitude to both my families for allowing me to tell their stories as part of mine, and for their openhearted support and assistance in the production of this book. I also thank Lisa for her love and patience during the process.

I am indebted to Saroj Sood for her contribution to my life as well as her help with the book, and to Soumeta Medhora. I would also like to thank Cheryl and Rochak for the help they provided, and especially Swarnima for being so giving of her time and for her friendship.

Finally, I would like to thank Andrew Fraser at Sunstar Entertainment for his guidance; Larry Buttrose, Ben Ball, and Michael Nolan at Penguin Australia; and Kerri Kolen at Penguin USA.

Born in Khandwa, Madhya Pradesh, India, **Saroo Brierley** lives in Hobart, Tasmania, where he manages a family business, Brierley Marine, with his father. Saroo's story has been published in several languages and is now a major motion picture from the Weinstein Company.